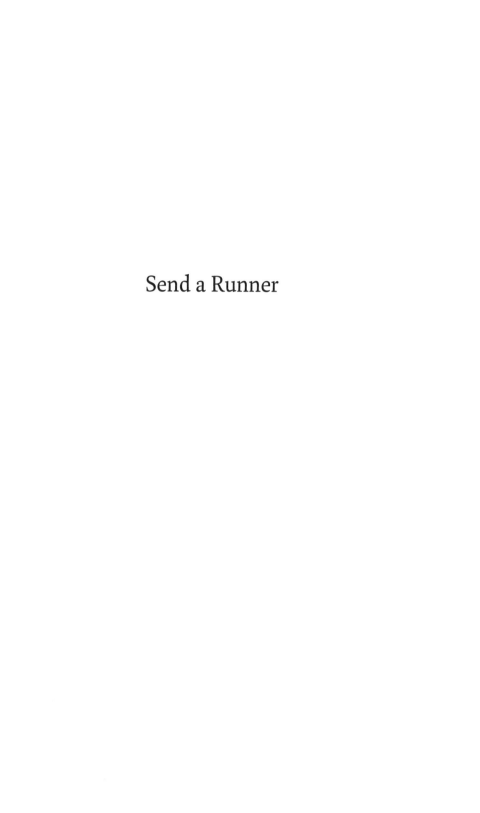

Send a Runner

Also by Jim Kristofic

Navajos Wear Nikes: A Reservation Life

The Hero Twins: A Navajo-English Story of the Monster Slayers

*Black Sheep, White Crow and Other Windmill Tales:
Stories from Navajo Country*

*Medicine Women: The Story of the First
Native American Nursing School*

Reservation Restless

SEND A RUNNER

A Navajo Honors the Long Walk

EDISON ESKEETS AND **JIM KRISTOFIC**

University of New Mexico Press | Albuquerque

ISBN 978-0-8263-6233-9 (cloth)
ISBN 978-0-8263-6234-6 (electronic)

Library of Congress Cataloging-in-Publication data is on file with the Library of Congress.

Cover photograph: Edison running with the country spread out toward Ganado Mesa.
Photo by Jason Bunion.
Frontispiece: Edison Eskeets, the runner, sitting in front of Hubbell Trading Post
in Ganado, Arizona. Photo by Joseph Kayne.
Designed by Felicia Cedillos
Composed in Huronia Navajo

Edison Eskeets:
For the Great Ones, we survived, we sing, we speak,
we dance into our journey as one.

Jim Kristofic:
For all the families who never got to come home,
we hold you dearly and we bring you with us.

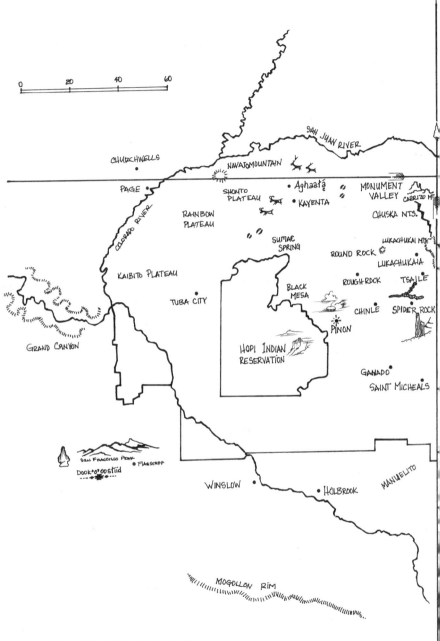

Map of *Diné Bikéyáh*, Navajo Country.
Courtesy of Nolan Karras James.

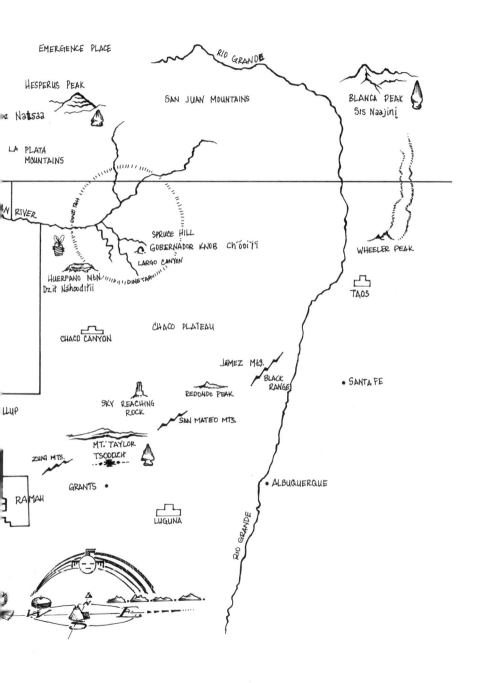

EMERGENCE PLACE

HESPERUS PEAK

e Natsaa

LA PLATA
MOUNTAINS

RIO GRANDE

SAN JUAN MOUNTAINS

BLANCA PEAK
Sis Naajiní

N RIVER

DINÉTAH

SPRUCE HILL
GOBERNADOR KNOB   Ch'óol'į́'į́

LARGO CANYON

WHEELER PEAK

HUERFANO MTN.
Dził Náhoodiłii

DINÉTAH

TAOS

CHACO PLATEAU

CHACO CANYON

JEMEZ Mts.

BLACK
RANGE

• SANTA FE

LLUP

SKY REACHING
ROCK

REDONDO PEAK

SAN MATEO MTS.

MT. TAYLOR
TSOODZIŁ

ZUNI MTS.

RAMAH

GRANTS •

LUGUNA

• ALBUQUERQUE

RIO GRANDE

Frontier Map with Route. Cartography by Capt. Allen Anderson, 5th US Infantry, Acting Engineer Officer, 1864. The line indicates the path of Edison Eskeets during the run in the summer of 2018.

Rug woven by Mary Henderson Begay for Edison Eskeets, the runner.
Photo by Edison Eskeets.

Heya, he weya, he yaha,
Ena heyana heya ha.
If you go to Navajoland,
If you go to Navajo, yes.

If you go to Navajoland,
Take your shroud,
Because death over there
Is firm and without doubt.[1]

—EIGHTEENTH CENTURY SPANISH FOLK SONG
FROM TAOS, NORTHERN NEW MEXICO

✛ DAY ONE

He is in the place where it started and continues. He is in the prayers.

The sun is coming. Blue shadows weave between dark branches of piñon and juniper.

Stars glitter in the cold morning sky. Edison Eskeets walks to the edge of the sandstone cascade called Canyon de Chelly. He offers his hand to the East.

His untied black hair streaks with gray. It falls around his thin, defined body. His high cheekbones and articulate nose give him a certain handsome nobility. He stands five feet, nine inches and weighs no more than 135 pounds.

He wears only a woven kilt and a pair of moccasins.

He looks through a half-mile of space to *Tsé ya'aa'hí* (Spider Rock), the sacred spire where *Na'ashjé'ii Asdzą́ą́* (Spider Woman) is said to have lived after teaching the art of weaving to the Diné—the Navajo people. Edison has painted his bare arm and chest white and offers the white corn from the *jish* (medicine pouch). His left arm is painted turquoise. His right leg is yellow and red. His left leg is black. The story is quiet. It is in the paint. It speaks of mountains, of a journey through the worlds, through forms and bodies, to this world with the help of the gods.

He looks to the remaining stars of the Milky Way and sees a specific curving shape. It is a feather, clear to any eye. It is what he needs. It is enough.

Edison was a quiet teenager at Gallup High School who spent more time herding sheep than talking to girls. He got recruited and became a first-team All-American runner for Haskell University. He ran professionally for years. He organized running camps all over the Reservation. Now he is the trader at Hubbell Trading Post, the oldest operating trading post in *Diné Bikéyah* (Navajo country). Today he will begin a run to honor the survivors of the Long Walk—the forced removal of most of the Diné people to a military-controlled reservation on the Pecos River in south-central New Mexico. He will run from here, Spider Rock, to Santa Fé—where the scheme for the Long Walk was drawn out and executed—to deliver a message. He will run 330 miles in fifteen days. He will run a marathon a day. He is fifty-nine years old.

Edison's prayers fall into the air like white cornmeal and become part of something that might be so old only Spider Woman remembers it.

The medicine needs to be gathered. People need healing. They send a runner. This morning, Edison is running.

Francisco de Coronado leaves Compostela in Mexico in 1540, envisioning the metals that will add to the Spanish treasury and to his own legacy. He takes over three hundred foot soldiers. He hires over a thousand Indian soldiers with promises of plunder in the north that will make their fortunes. He equips five hundred war horses, each with a coat of mail, and an armored cavalry soldier. The soldiers bring their wives and children. This is customary.

The party is easy to track. Hundreds of cattle and sheep bring up the rear as food.

The Spanish explorers grasp and steal up the Río San Pedro. They reach the Pecos River and follow it to what is now called the New Mexico border with Texas. There, they meet a people they call Querechos—plains Apaches—and Coronado says they are "one of the best bodies of any people I have seen in the Indies." One of Coronado's lieutenants writes that they do not eat human flesh, that they are gentle people, that they are "faithful friends."[2]

Edison makes it happen in the old way. He sets down a rug woven by Mary Henderson Begay in the pattern that explains why he is here. Against the gray background, you will see the blue and red lines of the rainbow, constellations of stars, the line of sky and atmosphere that protects Mother Earth, where meteorites are burned and destroyed, the plants that are medicine and food and dye for the rug. The plant *is* a rug and the rug is the plant. The white eagle feather. The *X* of the treaty. The dates of the Long Walk, 1864–1868, in brown wool. The sacred mountains. The four directions. It is all there. As a comfort. To protect us. It is the whole Navajo story. The story of the struggle for happiness.

Edison lays the rug on the ground as the *ya'sikaad* (ground cover). Edison gives her a carefully wrapped buckskin pouch of corn pollen. Two hundred years ago, these pouches would be made of hides of deer unpunctured by arrows or spears. They had to be killed by runners, who would chase the deer to exhaustion, where it could no longer run. They would pin the deer, take the sacred *tádídíín* (corn pollen) in their hands, and use it to smother the deer. Life became death and became Life. It is all so simple that it takes your whole life to understand.

Edison sets down the basket and puts the yellow corn pollen inside. He turns to his family. They are going to travel with him. His sister, Lorraine, will be his nurse, his coach, his advisor, and his provider, as she has been on many of his other runs. Her husband, Jason, and their daughter, Jay-Lynn, will drive ahead of him as he runs.

They are his bloodline, his family. He has children, but they are not here. But there are guests: journalists, politicians, executive directors, and well-wishers.

Edison speaks to them all the same. He takes up the *tádídíín,* and to each person he hands the blessing of the pollen. He tells them *Díí ní doleel.*

This is for your future. Your blessings for your path of life.

In all this he keeps it together. He stays focused. After the last blessing, he turns back to the sunrise. He sees the white band of dawn. And he just breaks down. He feels the old places and the old faces of the people who once lived in the canyon. You spot the ruins of the *Anasazi*

(Old People) in the broad, south-facing arches in the canyon walls. Some are impossibly mortared against the smooth, peach-colored sandstone. The *tł'oh 'azihii* (ephedra) blooms green, and the *t'iis* (cottonwood trees) spread in arteries of green fire at the canyon bottom.

The Diné call this place *Tseyí* (The Rock in the Canyon). It has called people into it for five thousand years. On the Colorado Plateau, it is the place where people have lived longest, through war, slaving, and drought. The people get labeled according to dates of occupation. They are silent and cannot complain. Archaic (2500–2000 BC), Basketmaker (200 BC–750 AD), and Anasazi, the builders who made the compounds and kivas (750 – 1300 AD).

The scholar and mythologist Joseph Campbell once said there were two great sacred spiritual centers he'd experienced in his long life. One was Chartres cathedral in France. The other was Canyon de Chelly. He called it "the most sacred place on earth."

When the Anasazi build the first kivas, a tribe on the other side of the planet that calls itself the *Achaeans*—who Americans will call the Ancient Greeks and who will lay the foundations of a civilization that will come to lay borders on this ground—emerge from a mass of fifty-one thousand square miles of dry ground and mountains. The Anasazi claim a country of similar size, stretching from modern central Arizona to southern Colorado.

Most Anasazi move away from Canyon de Chelly, but Hopi migrate through to hunt and farm the reliable flowing waters. The Diné moved in with sheep and horses in the 1700s. Or they were always here. They say one of the first Navajo clans—the *Tséńjíkinii* (Honey Comb Rock Clan)—emerged from the cliffs near what is now called the White House Ruin.

The Diné had one generation watching the corn pollen drifting in the cool sunrise and the peach trees shimmering green in the noon heat. Then the wars were on. With other tribes, with the New Mexicans, with the Americans. Then the government in 1931 stepped in to "preserve this record of human history" of the fight over plants and water.

At the Spider Rock overlook, a juniper twists dead into the sky. A lone naked limb is covered in graffiti. Someone has carved a marijuana leaf. The most common phrase knifed into the bark is "I Love the Rez." Brown sagebrush lizards dart between the roots of the tree.

Edison feels the movement of Spider Woman. He feels the direction of Mary Henderson Begay, the weaver.

He lets himself break down. He has finished the words that needed to be said. Many people don't know the traditions of the Navajo runner. They are lost. But they see it come back there that morning in front of *Tsé ya'aa'hí*—Spider Rock.

Edison starts running. He goes the first mile in his moccasins. He knows it is all already done.

He is thirty-one years old when he sails the Atlantic waters from Córdova in Spain to Mexico. He accompanies Archbishop Moya y Contreras and is made an officer of the Inquisition. He makes his money by loosing the scythes of cattle on the sparse land and firing his musket to make it so wolves howl no more in that country. He murders one of his servants, another Spaniard, and for this the magistrate says he must pay a heavy fine. He will not pay and flees to Nueva Vizcaya. He decides to equip an expedition of fourteen soldiers, a priest, and 115 animals to walk into the north country to find places where he can recover silver ore and his reputation. He lends some benevolence to the expedition when he claims he will look for two priests left behind by a mining expedition up the Río Grande.

No person in this new country knows that he is Antonio Espejo. In the winter of 1583, Espejo's men pick their way around Cebolleta Mesa. The mesa rises and connects with a pyramidal mountain rising by shield and escarpment, that from a distance shines blue as turquoise. A group of Indians has been tracking the Spaniards' movements from between the pines and come down from this mountain by way of a stream to meet Espejo at a small lake now called Laguna, New Mexico. Here, they trade. Espejo describes the natives as *Indios Cerranos*—mountain Indians. Some of the warriors wear the pelts of mountain lions. The men watch the horizon calm and alert as the long-eared deer of this new country.

De Espejo ranges as far west as the Hopi villages. There, one of his men is given a slave woman. This woman is an *India Cerrana*. They leave Hopi without incident and have nearly reached the Río Grande by the late spring. When passing through the country near Acoma, the slave woman escapes with another woman. They run to Acoma. The Spaniards chase them. The Acoma people and the nearby *Indios Cerranos* stand in front of the Spanish guns and fire arrows at the men in armor. De Espejo commands his men to give the women up. They stamp to the river and retreat south.

These *Indios Cerranos* are Navajos. Diné. And they have now become part of this thing called *history*.[3]

By 7:49 a.m., Edison has run more than eight miles.

I find him sitting in a folding camp chair. He bites at a half-banana and sips water in a blue T-shirt. The shirt features a silk-screen graphic of a man running. It is a picture his daughter drew of him years ago while he was running in the mountains near *Tsíma'* (Chama, New Mexico). Below the image, the shirt reads: "The Message 2018." He wears yellow-lensed sunglasses to fend off glare from the road. A ripstop woven cap keeps his ears and scalp from overheating. He got the cap at the K-Mart in Santa Fe. Blue Light Special.

"Nike is supposed to get us some running attire. But we're still waiting on it. So let's just go," Lorraine, his sister, says.

"This guy is a dancer out there," I say. "*Yá'áát'ééh.*" There is the tradition of the token. I give him a rock from *Dook'o'oosłiid*, the sacred mountain of the West. I have tied bluebird feathers to it. Edison gives me piki bread thin as rolled lizard skin.

I met Edison when I worked as a park ranger on the Navajo reservation several years ago. He knows I grew up in Ganado, Arizona. That I love the Navajo country and people, that I have attended and aided in ceremonies. He has shown me some of the traditions over the years. He knows I understand pain, as I have remained an athlete, that I still lift weights and help run a Brazilian jiu-jitsu school. He knows I write and so he invites me to bear witness to the run and to help. That is why I am here.

He adjusts his simple black shorts. His white woven Nikes with blue trim and blue swooshes have already begun to show some wear from running downhill on the asphalt.

The heat makes the road shimmer, and everyone's sweat is running. The thermometer in Jason and Lorraine's Nissan SUV reads over ninety-five degrees.

"Oh, this thing is a life saver," Edison says. He has tied a red bandana to his wrist for wetting his mouth. "Every time."

Edison is running two miles at a time to conserve energy in the heat. He asks for the rattle. His sister hands him a black-headed rattle. Edison shakes it and feels the comfort. He's been running with it since Spider Rock. While he ran, two different dogs chased after him, ready to sink their fangs into his hamstrings. But they listened to the rattle.

"The one dog coming after me, I just shook that rattle and he slunk back away," Edison says. "He knew."

Everyone laughs.

"Let's go another two," he says.

Jason asks, "How do you feel?"

"Tired." Edison smiles. "Join me."

He runs another two miles. We stop to rest beside the road. The chair comes out. The water.

"As you run, your mind starts to get simple," he says. "You'll see. When we get six more miles, start asking me some math problems." He laughs.

I say it's a lot of suffering.

"It is. That's exactly what it is. Can you imagine what they had to go through during the Long Walk? To make it? Just unbelievable."

Edison runs past shacks with satellite dishes. Past parked vans next to pallets stacked as improvised corral panels.

His hair drifts down to the direct point between his shoulder blades as he runs past a rolling set of dunes where the stumps of decapitated tamarisk trees rise from the sand. The American government had planted the thin, reedy tamarisk tree to control erosion in the West. The tree kept rivers from shifting by armoring their banks with thick roots. So the force of the river eroded down and gullied the water table, making all floods new creators of drought.

The tamarisk come from an older world. They grew along the

battlefields of the Trojan War. The tree is a survivor by being a ruthless killer.

They take up salt out of the soil and store it in their thin needles. When they drop their needles in the autumn, they coat the soil with layers of saline that eliminate any seedlings that are not tamarisk. The seeds survive fire. When removal crews try to burn them out, they grow from the ashes.

The trees had evolved past the government's best policies. They are—actually—an expression of the policy: we are taking over. We are all that will be. Clear the road.

The tribal government wants the trees gone. And they are removing them. The Navajos have done their own exterminating here.

Edison runs with arms at the angle a hawk makes before it leaps to flight. He runs up on a man jogging beside the road under the cottonwood trees and sweating through his gray T-shirt. The man's belly bounces as he strikes hard on the pavement. He huffs to Edison, "You're going too fast!"

Edison passes him.

"How far are you running?" the man asks.

"330 miles."

"What?"

Edison cannot reply. He is already too far ahead.

The Acoma people call themselves *Haak'u*. They and the Navajo seem to know something that had escaped the notice of the largest tribes in Mexico: that the Spanish are not gods and are simply invading men who can die by violence.

They learn this with the visit of Antonio Espejo, long before Juan de Oñate tries to found a capital for the Spanish in 1599 at Yunque Yungue pueblo (the modern day Ohkay Owingeh, New Mexico) where the *Ts'í'ma'* (Chama River) meets *To' Bi'aad* (the Río Grande).[4] The Diné and other *Indios apaches* hit the settlement so often that the colonists petition the viceroy in Mexico to allow them to return to New Spain. The viceroy says no.

The Diné attack from the horse. They drive the Spanish colonists thirty miles south to a settlement called Santa Fé de Granada—modern day Santa Fé. So if you want to know why Santa Fé is the capital, those Navajo warriors give you the answer.

The Spanish claim the country in the name of God. The Navajos test God.

The Diné ride into Jémez pueblo in 1639 and kill the priest there. They wait for God's answer.

Sixteen years later, a patrol of nineteen Spaniards arrives at the Sky City of Acoma in the expanse of a desert valley. Giants of sandstone buttes stand to the sky. The tallest of these rocks rises over 350 feet in the air. Here the Acomans stacked their sandstone houses and protected them with mud plaster. Holes in the rock travel down more than thirty feet and trap water for the *Haak'u*. The people use the nearby aquifer to grow corn, squash, beans, and melons.

The Spanish—led by Juan de Zaldívar, Oñate's favorite nephew— decide to take these things while on a trip to Zuni to meet his uncle. The *Haak'u* will have none of it. They invite the Spanish to the top. They give them water. A leader named Zutucapán smiles and tours the Spaniards around the village. Then Acoma warriors grab them and knife them. Five Spaniards decide to commit suicide by leaping from the rocks. One dies, but four survive by hitting a soft dune of windblown sand. The Acomans are great runners. They make the mistake of allowing these men to flee and bring news of what happened.[5]

Oñate sends the brother of the slain commander to take revenge. When the force of seventy men rides between the towering sandstone at Acoma, they find the *Haak'u* joined by hundreds of *Indios Cerranos*— Navajos—and other Apaches under a chieftain named Bempol, jeering and screaming defiance from the cliffs above.[6] Bempol is a Navajo and his warriors have come down from the Blue Mountain that rises in the north to help the *Haak'u* and so they do not miss a chance to kill these filthy invaders.[7]

The Spaniards fight for two days. Arrows slice the air. Rocks rip cartilage and crush skulls. Lead balls pop through bodies and dead men fall from the cliffs. The Spanish get two cannons to the top of the rock. They fire two hundred balls. The *Haak'u* and the Navajo do not care. They run into the nightmare of fire and smoke with war clubs and stone knives. Their corpses—along with any women and children the Spanish can put to the sword—pile to over eight hundred. Any wood in the village is put to the torch.

In a spirit of revenge, Zaldívar stages a butchering of the surviving warriors and has their pieces thrown from Sky City. He marches over seventy warriors and nearly five hundred women and children back to Santo Domingo pueblo to stand in a thing called "a trial."

Oñate passes sentence on February 12. The men are all to be slaves or cripples. If you look over twenty-five years old, the Spanish take you to a cottonwood chopping block and hack off one of your feet with an ax. People debate that only the toes of the feet were chopped off. Take your pick. Then you serve twenty years as a slave. If you are a boy who looks younger than twenty-five, you are sold as a slave. If you are a woman, you are sold as a slave. If you are a girl, you are marched south to a convent in Mexico and you disappear. If you are a boy, you are given to Zaldívar, the man who commanded the death of your father and uncles, and he spills water over your head in something called a "baptism" and you are told you are this thing called a "Wet Head," a "Christian."

Two Hopis are found among the people. They are spared this sentence. Oñate only asks that their right hands are cut off. They are sent back to Hopi as a warning. They run.

Records report that the new governor of New Mexico in 1609 sends Oñate back to Mexico, where he is tried and convicted for his many atrocities, including those against the *Haak'u* and the Diné, that he is forever banished from New Mexico. There is no record of those boys and girls being released from slavery. For the next 250 years, Navajo people will be recorded in the Catholic baptismal records more than any other tribe.

Edison runs the two miles to the Denny's parking lot. When he stops, he yells, "Whew!" like a war whoop. He shakes the rattle. Now the sit in the camping chair. He takes his shoes off and wets his feet and legs. Lorraine pours cool water in his hat.

"Wow. I can taste the salt coming down," he says. He takes down half a banana and a half-handful of sunflower seeds. He sips water. Always the small sips.

"You can't take too much," he says. "You don't want to gulp down and have that air bubble in your system. It feels awful. You've really got to regulate."

Lorraine points to his legs. "Look! It's the feather!"

Edison saw a feather pattern in the stars along the Milky Way that morning. Now it is on his leg. I see it, too, in the yellow lines on the red.

"Oh wow. There it is," he says. "And this paint job was just slap and dash. I put the paint on in the dark."

So the feather is there. Edison and his sister talk about it in Navajo. The more fatigued Edison becomes, the more Navajo he speaks. He swears he remembers there was half a banana stowed away. There is. Jason laughs. "You've still got it together."

Edison gets up out of his chair and saunters over to the sidewalk and sticks out his thumb like he's hitchhiking. It's a joke. But it's also a reality. He often hitchhiked over twenty miles to his home near Springstead, New Mexico, after his cross-country practices at Gallup High School.

He steps out of the Denny's parking lot to the road. He runs two miles past Chinle High School, past the Navajo Tribal Utility Authority (NTUA) building, past a mural featuring a chieftain named Manuelito that says: "Honor Your Life."

He stops and sits in the folding chair. He shakes the black gourd rattle.

"I need this."

Jason nods and says, "It takes it. It takes it."

"It takes the pain," Edison says. "When we're done, I'm going to sell this on eBay."

Jason laughs and hands Edison water.

He crosses his legs and points at the paint running down to his socks.

"This is what you call *chizhí*." Everyone laughs. In Navajo, *chizhí* means something rough, like firewood. When your skin is dry and flaky, a Navajo will say, "I am just *chizhí*," in the way an African American person might say, "I'm all *ashy*."

"When you sell that rattle," Jason says, "you'll have to sign it *From Chizhí Boy*."

Edison laughs. He changes his socks and Lorraine checks his toenails. They are starting to loosen on two of his toes. He goes another two miles.

He runs past a mural on a utility shed next to the gas company that reads: "Diné Bikéyah." He passes two teenagers carrying skateboards.

He rests in the gas station parking lot. He goes another two miles to the base of the long hill leading out of the Chinle valley.

Edison stops. "It's tough. It's just disastrous. With the terrain uneven like this, you have to really watch your stepping. It's like your mind is taking every step for you. And that really tires you out. I can do the run. The run is not the problem. It's the road."

He has run over twenty miles today. I timed his runs and he was running each mile at a little under seven minutes. His breathing comes even, like he has walked.

"I can feel the fatigue. It came from that noontime. That's when The Zap hits you. Once that happens, you can feel it three hours later. That's when you really get tired. So I've just been taking as much salt as I can. I've been eating sunflower seeds like a bird."

He looks to the long hill. He clucks his tongue.

The Keres and Tewa-speaking people are not like the Diné. They try living with the Spaniards and their way of life called *feudalism*. They engage in a new cruel ceremony called *taxation* and must furnish a cotton blanket or tanned deerskin each year just for the privilege of having been conquered. Some people take up Christianity in hopes that they will not be enslaved, which is illegal. They are often enslaved. A Franciscan missionary writes how soldiers clear out the natives' larders of food. The natives starve so badly that they eat charcoal and ashes. Some run to the mountains. The Diné take them in. The refugees never stop coming.

The Diné do not know the word "illegal." There is no need for it here. There is only the advantage of taking the small, wooly *dibé* (sheep), who perform the miracle of picking the roughest grass into their mouths and whose bodies sculpt meat and wool to feed and clothe the People. And then there is *łįį*—the miracle animal of the horse. The Diné discover their humming strength and straddle their speed to raid the pueblos and the Spanish in the long war of attrition.

A Spanish colonist named Juan Martínez de Montoya is the first to feel this from his stolen lands near *Dziłzhiin* (Jémez Mountains). The Navajo raiders take up the warfare like a vocation. They make prayers. They develop stalking songs. They paint their moccasins with snakes to make their feet move quickly and silently. The *łįį* carries them into this new destiny.

Within a decade, they are attacking on horseback the headquarters Oñate established at the confluence of the Río Grande and Chama rivers. The natives at Jémez pueblo are allied with the Spanish. The Diné ride down on them. Within twenty years, the Jémez people have allied with the Diné.

Edison and Lorraine debate whether they want to run up the hill. It will be difficult to stay on the edge of the road in the thickening traffic driving south to the homesteads around Ganado, Piñon, and Burnside.

Edison also feels things falling off.

"It felt like my body was extending into the ground," he said later. "Like my energy was just being sucked into the ground. In Navajo you'd say, "*Nihokáá'góó áhoot'éii áhóodziil.* My feet are becoming the earth. But it wasn't a good thing. It needed some adjustment."

It is decided to begin with the hill tomorrow in the morning, when the traffic is much lighter.

Jason ties a strip of neon-pink marker tape to the barbed-wire fence where we have stopped. Edison will begin the run from there.

Edison walks past my car and admires Rainey, my Staffordshire bull terrier in the back seat. Rainey licks his face through the gap in the window. We shake hands and he sits inside the SUV to ride back with his family to rest and recover for tomorrow. He shakes the rattle. It carries Edison's pain. And so much else. And so much more to come.

Jason lowers the back door of the black Nissan SUV. The silver letters along its edge reveal the name of the model: Armada.

The Diné earn a name for themselves. A Franciscan named Alonso de Benavides cobbles together an adobe hut near the native village now called Santa Clara to serve as a mission to these mountain people. He has been told by Tewa-speaking people that these mountain people are "Apaches de Nebawhoo"—Apaches Who Keep Large Planted Fields. They are Apaches who have learned the planting songs and corn ceremonies from the refugees. They live where lightning pounds the slopes of mountains. The Spanish colonists start calling them "Navájos."

And though they have taken to the *gish* (digging stick) and the singing for rains, Benavides calls them "the most warlike of the entire Apache nation" and that they have "proven to be the crucible of Spanish valor." Navajos mostly test "Spanish valor" when the Spanish colonists ride out or ask their Puebloan allies to ride out and steal Navajo women and children for their slave market. This happens after the Spanish run out of slaves in the Río Grande regions.

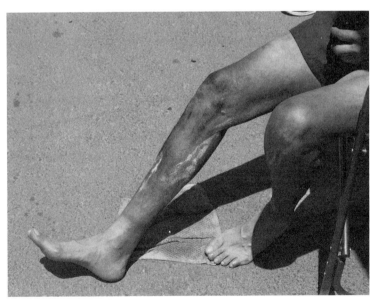

Edison resting after running out of Canyon de Chelly Tribal Park.
The yellow paint on his leg has shaped a feather pattern. Chinle, Arizona.
Photo by Jim Kristofic.

Slaves become an abundant resource. When one of the governors of New Spain is accused of kidnapping two girls from their pueblo, he defends himself by asking why he would do this when he was able to simply give away more than a hundred Apache captives earlier that year.

Benavides puts this new name—Navájo—down in his book titled *Memorial to the King of Spain* in the year 1630 at the mission in Santa Clara. It will be a place to convert these new Navajo people.[8]

The Navajos never show up.

They stay in the mountains. They come down to take horses from men who would use those mounts to ride out and enslave them. Perhaps some believe they are liberating the *łįį* from lives of depredation and inviting them to epics of conquest and vengeance against the oppressors. When they speak with Puebloan peoples, they tell them to rebel, to live free to sing their corn songs, and call to the eagles in their dances.

People report seeing the Diné raiding villages on the Great Plains in a place now called on maps "western Kansas."

At six o'clock the next morning, Edison stands at the edge of the road in a black Nike windbreaker. That box of supplies from Nike has arrived. He shakes the rattle.

"I need this," he says. "It's a comfort. I think about those people in that walk. Many of them suffered. Many did not make it. They died of exhaustion. Dehydration. Stress and fatigue. They'd needed comfort. I'm here now. I'm alive. Remembering them. That's what the rattle was for in a medicine way. During the healing ceremony, it would bring the patient comfort, would ease the pain. It was a way for the great ones, the deities, to communicate through the medicine man."

Trucks drive past and honk at him. Drivers lean out and pump their fists in approval. The running life is strong in *Diné Bikéyah*. Edison shakes the rattle to signal the drivers. On the approach to the hill, he steps off the road, and the Armada pulls off with him. Edison feels his feet slipping. He sits in the folding chair while Lorraine changes his shoes to a pair of red-and-black Avias with new inserts.

Edison sips Sobé water. He needs the sodium. When The Zap comes, it's all about the salt.

He laughs, "Oh, whose idea *was* this? Who came up with this? *Man,* this is terrible."

Then up he goes.

I once heard that Navajo runners would train by running up hills with water in their mouths to force themselves to develop a strong breath.

Edison's arms seem to fly him up the hill.

Someone sends a runner. Plans swirl out from Taos. The runners carry cords tied with three knots. The revolt happens almost simultaneously in every village.

Farmers and builders of rock houses hang and stone priests to death. In northern New Mexico they execute these tasks efficiently.

Edison running the hill out of the Chinle Valley. Photo by Jay-Lynn Bunion.

Only one soldier of hundreds survives. In four days, the native people have killed over four hundred of the two thousand four hundred colonists.

Everyone flees to Santa Fé. Governor Antonio de Otermín limps with the survivors to El Paso and then back to Mexico. He blames it all on the Apache and the Apaches de Navajo, those mountain puppet masters promoting rebellion by day and stealing horses by night.

This is all supposed to be against God's plan. A Spanish historian, Juan Armando Niel, claims that the Puebloan people and the Apaches de Navajo had invoked a kind of Satanic climate change that caused a nine-year drought and brought a rain of ashes for seven years before the rebels' "stubborn, insolent apostasy was confirmed."[9]

The Spanish will not accept this. They are back in force by the fall of 1692. They are led by a new governor, Diego de Vargas Zapata y Luján. Vargas does not mess around. When he hits pueblos, he has his soldiers baptize the prisoners to save their souls and then they hack their heads from their bodies. He establishes himself at Santa Fé. He asks for reinforcements from Mexico. He wants convicts from the Mexican jails sent up to be teachers and miners.

He rides out and persuades the survivors in the pueblo villages to cooperate. Jémez Pueblo, set in its crags of the dark mountains, defies him. During Vargas's visit there is another group of people staying outside the pueblo. They are Navajos.

Vargas leaves the next day to threaten Acoma and Zuni. He takes the long way around to avoid the country of the Navajos.

Vargas arrives at Acoma with an army of nearly ninety men. The Acoma elders inform Vargas that they are now allied with the Navajos. They say the Navajos have seen how the Spanish cut hands from wrists, how they hang men and carry women into slavery. The Diné live in the moment, but their memories are long. So are the *Haak'u*. Vargas gets the feeling the Acoma people are talking with him in order to give them time for the Navajo to arrive and trap his army.

He leaves early.

He is welcomed at Zuni. That night, Navajos steal sixteen of his horses.

Vargas reaches Hopi. He is met by a thousand Hopi warriors. The Navajos have ridden ahead of him and warned the Hopi. He travels back to Zuni. He learns that the Navajos penalized Zuni by taking nine of their horses. Vargas does not pause for vengeance. He and his men ride straight for El Paso. Navajos kill two of them.

Within a year, Vargas returns with ten times more men. He sacks and burns his way to Jémez. He destroys the village and captures three hundred and sixty-one women and children.

Edison ascends the hill as though it were level ground.

"I just can't keep this going. Never again. This is the last time," he whispers beside the road after he stops at the two-mile mark.

Edison has run worse hills. Lorraine remembers how—during one of his ultraruns that took him through Chama—Edison had to run seven miles up a mountain through freezing rain. Then it turned to snow.

Then, during their evening run, they heard a Bigfoot. The massive, bear-like primate screamed at them.

"It was just out of nowhere," Edison says. "So loud. I could not compare it to a human sound."

"And you screamed back!" Lorraine laughs.

"Yeah," Edison says. "In the traditional way, you're taught not to let anything startle you. You have to get aggressive back. So I did. I did my job."

We have emerged from the Chinle valley onto the high, grassy plain running south between Balakai Mesa and Beautiful Valley. The plain runs flat for seven miles directly to the junction of Burnside. The road is almost perfectly straight. The grass bends yellow and green. The wind is always alive. Edison runs into it for twelve miles.

Then we break for Edison to rest and Jason ties the neon-pink marker tape to the barbed-wire fence beside the road.

The revolt comes that summer. Taos, Picurís, the Tewas, Santo Domingo, and Cochití kill five missionaries and twenty-one Spaniards. When the bloodletting is done, they leave their kivas and run for the mountains. The Navajos take them in. The Puebloans teach the Navajos stories, weaving, and ceremonies. It is the start of war with the Spanish that will last three lifetimes. For the Navajos, the revolt will never stop.

By the end of the summer of 1696, the Spanish execute five men at Acoma. They sell more than eighty women and children into slavery to replace their numbers in the colony. The people at Zuni join the Spanish. Now only the Hopi, the Apaches, and the Navajo have a chance of breaking the fingers of the Spanish's clutch on the ground.

The Zuni—now vassals to Spain—named the people "Apaches" long ago and the Spanish adopt the name. It means "the enemies."[10]

That afternoon, a red-tailed hawk follows Edison every two miles. It often watches from a telephone pole.

The sun pounds the earth. Jay-Lynn makes a joke about how she is getting sunburned only on her right side, which is why they call this place "Burnside."

Edison runs and breaks in the shade. *'Azee' ntł'iní* (scarlet globemallow) grows in velvet-green and sunset-orange between the cracks in the blacktop. He sips water.

"I said to Jay-Lynn, my niece, 'You might have the best ultramara-thoner in the country here with you right now.' I would train for this and . . . well, let me explain . . . let's say you go for a run and you do something like four or five miles. And you say, 'I'm really going to push hard. And I'm going to make a better time.' And let's say you do that. You'll likely lose a pound of weight. Maybe. What I'm doing, I'll run during the day and lose seven pounds in a stretch. Seven pounds. I tell that to these interviewers from *Runner's World* or other people. They don't believe me. And I think, 'The wrong person is doing the interview.' It's all about levels. When you start at a certain level. Then you go up. Then up a level. Then up a level. Now I'm here."

He holds his hand high above his head.

"Who do you talk to about that?"

Two more miles.

It was 1981, and he was on a sixteen-mile training run in Kansas. He could feel himself lengthening out. His legs were making that perfect extension with his stride called "leading the charge." Then he heard a voice say, "Hey. I'm over here." And he thought it was strange, so he kept running. He kept leading the charge with perfect clarity. Then the voice came again. "I'm over here." And he stopped. Edison stepped to the edge of the road and walked down the shoulder. He thought maybe a home-less person needed help. Maybe someone had fallen alongside the road. Instead, he saw a little clover glowing green in the shade of a tree. The clover said, "Here I am. Thank you."

"I still think about that to this day," he says. "What *was* that?"

I ask if he's heard voices on this run so far.

"It's many things," he says. "It's so hard to say now. I'm picking up many emotions, many feelings. Right now it's like a tumbleweed just rolling around. There's many feelings. Frustration. Love. Anger. Someone died near here. Someone got married near here. It's like a tumbleweed, just spinning. That's how I know it's real. That people actually lived here."

Edison dances the rest of the twelve miles toward Burnside. The plan is to reach the junction by breakfast tomorrow and run the last five miles to the Hubbell Trading Post by one o'clock in the afternoon.

People will be waiting to witness Edison's run. The *Navajo Times* will interview him. They expect him to give a speech. He will try.

In the spring of 1705, two large Navajo war parties hit the corrals at San Juan, Santa Clara, and San Ildefonso pueblos. The Spanish gather over a hundred genízaros—nomadic Plains Indians whose people have been eaten by disease and violence and who have been adopted or perhaps enslaved into one of the pueblos—and march north and west and kill Navajos with the hope of enslaving the survivors.[11] These genízaros are a people without a country. They are a servant class, the men often working as herders and the women as concubines. They are the desperate poor with no family ties to land or wealth.[12] The common ground they inhabit often becomes a no-man's land of bloodshed and cruelty.[13] They travel into the San Juan mountains and capture two women. They learn one is Navajo and the other is from Jémez. They beat the women and torture them to find the location of nearby Navajo rancherías. These women must be mothers. They die before they talk.

A few days later, the Spanish captain rides up on one of his Pueblo warriors hitting a Navajo woman with clubs. The woman cries out to him and asks to be baptized. By this, she is asking to become a slave and perhaps live. The captain has her baptized. And then the Pueblo warriors beat her to death.[14]

That night, we eat pizza at Edison's housing at Hubbell Trading Post. Kari—one of the spirited staffers from Western National Parks Association—baked us a chocolate cake powdered with sugar. We dig in.

Edison lies on the sofa watching an old Western, like he's having a sick day from work. Contemporary paintings of pueblos and *yei* dancers hang on every wall. A plastic yogurt container now filled with ashes sits by Edison's sliding glass door for when he needs to bless the house or to pray.

He tells a story of Farmington, where Lorraine and her husband, Jason, live. They both work for Alpine Lumber and have worked in different lumber yards most of their lives.

"It's a really nice place, Farmington, I think," Edison says. "But it's too much weight there. A lot of racism. I got pulled over there one time. I had to ask the police, 'Why am I being stopped?' They asked me for my driver's license. Insurance card. I think they were just hoping to find *something.* I kept asking, 'Why am I being stopped?' And they never answered. They *never* answered."

I sense this is one interaction of many. I sense Edison and his family do not like cops.

Edison has found it difficult to straddle the world of art broker and local trader. An old man came in one day with a check for $1,500. The man had received the check in the mail, and Edison had to explain in Navajo that it was a clearinghouse-style scam that you should just throw away. But the old man must have needed the money. He brought it to the trading post and asked Edison to cash it.

"I have to explain, 'No, it's a scam. It's a promotional item. It's not real.' I'm saying all this in Navajo. So he nods and takes the check and walks out of the trading post. He sits outside. He comes back in and says he doesn't need me to cash the check. He understands. Instead, he asks for $1,500 worth of *items.*"

Lorraine chuckles. She understands the old man's problems. She is working a job she doesn't like in a place she doesn't love. It is all so her daughter can go to school there.

"We don't really go out much in Farmington," she says. "Just stay home. There really isn't any place to go there."

Lorraine tells me about their mother. She was a weaver who would weave designs out of her own memory. She'd take and sell them in Gallup and that's how they bought groceries. Their father was a janitor at Fort Wingate high school. Their mother didn't know English, but she could still weave the teachers' names into rugs for them, just by recognizing the symbols of the letters.

"Edison and I basically grew up the same. We didn't have no water. No electricity. Edison herded a lot of sheep. A lot. And he got into running on his own."

Edison used to work at A. C. Houston's lumber yard in Gallup. He would ride twenty-six miles on his bicycle to get to work and then ride twenty-six miles back.

Lorraine remembers learning English for the first time.

"Speaking only Navajo as our first language, I went to school for the first time. I had a black lady as my teacher and I've never seen a black person before. I thought, 'What is *wrong* with this person? Were they out in the sun too long?' I didn't know what she was talking about most of the time. Then I learned English and it got easier."

Their mother still has not learned functional English.

Edison rises to show me an old picture. Edison stands in his mid-thirties with solid black hair. His daughters crowd around him. They stand next to Jane Fonda.

In another photograph, he is standing under a small canopy in front of the Wings of America complex with three Anglo women. One is Doris Brown Heritage, the first female to clock a mile under five minutes. The other is Joan Behoit Samuelson, the first Olympic gold medalist in the 26.2 mile. The other is Mary Decker Slaney, who had run on the Olympic team four times and held records in all races from 800 meters to 10,000 meters. Edison called them and explained what he was trying to do as executive director of Wings of America—a nonprofit that uses running to teach Native American youth to feel pride in their culture and strive to succeed in the American world. Edison supervised over two dozen running and fitness camps in tribal communities across the Southwest. In the winter, coaches assembled teams of athletes to compete at the USA national cross-country championships. Over the past three decades, runners who train with Wings of America have won more than twenty national junior titles.

The champions showed up for him.

Edison blinks before his younger, smiling self.

"When you're that age," he sighs, "you just want to save everybody."

I ask if he'd thought about partnering with Wings for this run, that his runners might have joined him in the road and run behind him like a scene out of a *Rocky* movie.

He shakes his head. The organization had not responded to his emails or phone calls. Ties had been severed quietly out of Edison's thought. But those relationships were replaced with new ones. And new questions, mostly from his former students.

A painted mural of *Naʼashjéʼii Asdzą́ą́* (Spider Woman) on an abandoned cinder-block utility shed on the running route at the edge of Canyon de Chelly Tribal Park. Artist Unknown. Photo by Jim Kristofic.

"So many people have asked me, 'What's the meaning?' They are asking why I'm doing this. And I'm trying to explain to them that I don't fully know. It's so many things. Many voices. Many people. I don't know. But I think what it is about is Man. Man moving forward through time. Beyond that? We're out there dancing in the road.

"We're doing this now," he says. "But I'm thinking about the old ones. I'm looking toward the Great Ones. And the old ones. The ones who actually chiseled with language the songs and the dances that connect us to this place. I know it's here. I saw it in the stars. At Spider Rock. The feather from the *yaʼsikaad*."

Within twenty years, the French have entered the Plains and have met a buffalo-hunting tribe of horsemen who are called *Nuhmuhnuh* (The People). The French do not know these people are an empire in embryo who will become known as the *komantcia,* an insult often slung at them by the Utes. *Komantcia* means "Someone Who Wants to Fight Me All the Time." The Spanish will translate *komantcia* as *Comanche*.[15] They sell them guns better than any Spanish soldier will ever carry.[16] These people use the guns to join with the Utes and kill Navajos and Apaches. Or they sell them as slaves to the Spanish.

The Diné fly on the backs of their horses. They take livestock. They begin to own the ground. The Spaniards begin to refer to them disdainfully as *Los Dueños del Mundo*—Lords of the World. They ride offerings through the heart of Ute hunting grounds to a 14,100-foot mountain they call *Tsisnaajinii* (Where the Black Streak Extends). The mountain becomes as sacred as the sunrise.

The Diné begin to carve petroglyphs in the walls of Canyon de Chelly. Rather than scraping in the forms of Avanyu, the coiling horned serpent who brings the lightning and guards the water, or the hunchbacked Kokopeli, that clown who plays his flute for rain, the Diné are more documentarian. They carve riders coming into the canyon. The riders wear wide-brimmed hats. They carry swords and guns. They wear crucifixes.

The cool breeze fills the blue dawn. Edison takes the first two miles with no rattle over the grassy plain toward Burnside under the dome of sky. He doesn't sit down or rest. He'd spent years training his legs for this kind of run.

"I spent that time sort of getting more sores broke in," he says. "If I hadn't done that, it would be over. I wouldn't make it. No way."

Jason and Lorraine pull the Armada to the side of the road to photograph Edison running in front of horses grazing with a red mesa behind them. He runs past the green highway mile marker. It reads: 419.9 mile. When ADOT put up mile markers that read "420," the local kids kept stealing them to hang them in their bedrooms or at their favorite party spot in the desert.

Edison is running. He cruises past Balakai Mesa and Balakai Point. He takes the rattle. He runs past a Native American Church tipi set up in front of a stick-frame house barely larger than a storage shed.

The road man walks out of the tipi. Edison shakes the rattle and the road man raises both arms to Edison.

Jay-Lynn and Jason Bunion wait beside the Armada support vehicle
for Edison to start the run toward Ganado. Near Snake Flat, Arizona.
Photo by Lorraine Eskeets.

After he has run the twelve miles, we sit at breakfast in Burger King. Kari—the cheerful, perceptive woman who works for Western National Parks Association (WNPA)—has been helping with the fundraising for the run. She buys breakfast. Edison digs into his large coffee and his French-toast sticks. He is burning more than three thousand calories a day. He almost can't eat enough to cover the burn. Tonight he will need to wake in the middle of the night to eat.

He is somewhat sullen this morning.

"I was hoping the people in the tipi would have received the message, that I was coming," he says. "They break at night and someone would have noticed it. Then they would have all been out standing at the fence. But that didn't happen."

Whenever he sees the tipi set up, he considers the people inside. "That tipi, those ceremonies. They tell us we are all connected. We're all part of this circle."

He almost missed that circle. When he attended Gallup High School his freshmen year, his coach picked him out as a natural talent who had likely been well-conditioned herding goats and sheep over rocky terrain at 6,500-foot elevation. The coach turned out to be right. During tryouts, Edison blew the other runners away and was put on varsity. This meant longer school days. This meant hitchhiking home on some evenings. Most evenings.

He finished tenth at the 1976 New Mexico state cross-country championships his junior year. In his senior year, he was never recruited by any colleges because his cross-country coach left the school and they had to cancel their season. So Edison knew he wasn't going to college. He would work in a lumber yard or a stone yard and make money until something else came.

But someone had told Jerry Tuckwin about Edison. Tuckwin, a cross-country and track coach at Haskell Indian Junior College (now Haskell Indian Nations University) in Lawrence, Kansas, offered Edison a running scholarship and a free education.

Edison asked his mom if it would be okay to leave. She said no.

But he continued to ask her for permission until she saw something in him that needed to leave. So she said yes.

That August of 1978, Tuckwin drove through the Reservation to collect the new student athletes for that year. He saw Edison hesitating with his small bag and jean jacket at his home in New Mexico. He did not talk much. Tuckwin wasn't sure Edison would get on the bus. But Edison did.

While he was at Haskell, he was invited to a Tipi Way. He went with a Sioux friend of his. He was going okay with his running that year, but not great. He was restless and eager. The ceremony started. Edison took medicine and smoked tobacco. Everyone took a break at two in the morning. This is usually a time when the road man will begin to resolve the scenarios people bring in with them. During the break, an old man called Edison over. Edison saw the man had been sitting in a wheelchair. He had no legs.

"He says, 'You are a runner.' Now I didn't tell him this. Somehow he just knew. And he said, 'I know you're looking at me and you must feel bad for me. But don't. Because I'm a full man. I'm a full man. And for you, you are going to do well. You're going to be fine.'"

In the following cross-country season, Edison was ranked in the top six cross-country runners in the nation. He was the only American-born member of the All-American team. The people ranked above him were all foreigners recruited from overseas.

After high school, it's tough for Native runners, tough for them to make it. Edison recalls Andy Martínez from Acoma Pueblo, who ran a 4:10 mile as a freshman. Before the race, he was prepared by the women. They would say prayers over him and brush him with feathers. He would take an arrowhead in his mouth. And he would just blow everyone away. Stanford recruited him. But he decided to stay near Acoma and to work and start a family.

"He was amazing," Edison says. "He just blew everyone away. He could run that 4:10 mile as a *freshman*. I could never break a 4:17 mile. It's just my length of leg, the width of my hips. When I start to go fast, I wobble a little. I just don't have the body. I'm not anatomically there."

A man sitting near us in the Burger King stands up and groans. His belly pushes at the edge of his jeans and nearly swells over his rodeo-championship belt buckle. Paper whispers as he dumps his trash.

In the years when John Adams is thinking of whether there ought to be a Declaration of Independence and Virginia slave-owner Patrick Henry is thundering, "Give Me Liberty or Give Me Death!" on the other side of the ocean of grass, in the greener, wetter world of the British colonies, the Mexican colonies in the north must begin importing horses from Spain. The Navajos have captured most of them.[17]

The Mexicans begin to back down. The Navajo allow two priests to build missions at the foothills of *Tsoodził* at places they name Encinal and Cebolleta.[18]

Within sixty years, the Mexicans have their independence. They prove very good at enslaving Navajos. Or killing them. Then they recruit Navajos to kill away their own future by betraying their Apache allies.

The governor of Mexico calls a meeting with a group of southern Navajos and tells them if they march with the Spanish against their allies, the Apaches, they will get paid for every dead Apache. All they have to do is cut their heads off and show them. They promise one hundred pesos for each Apache captive. The Navajos ride out with Pueblo warriors from Laguna in the summer and kill forty Apaches.

Navajo leaders attend a council in Santa Fé so they can make a promise to continue the war. One persuasive argument comes from two Comanche chiefs who attend with the governor. They promise they will exterminate the Navajo people if they fail to hunt the Apaches. It is all a kill pact.

When the next slaving expedition rides out, less than thirty Navajos join. They will take their chances. One Navajo warrior joins and distinguishes himself as *Hashke Lik'izhi* (Spotted Warrior). He is given the title of general and a stipend from Mexico. The Apaches notice him, too. Apache warriors attack the home of *Hashke Lik'izhi*. He rides after them and an arrow takes him through the arm. A few days later, the wound has not healed, it puffs with infection, and he dies.[19]

Edison runs east to Ganado. He feels the heavy crosswinds. He takes off his hat and holds it in his fist. The wind tips him sideways but he recovers. It is the first time his family fears he may fall down. The maroon hills and peach-colored mesas roll up and down in approach to Hubbell Trading Post. Edison clocks seven-minute miles to the shade of the cottonwoods near the trading post turnoff. We are slightly delayed as Lorraine pulls ahead to get a shot of Edison. Edison takes water from his chair. He asks about the time. It is 2:30. We are due at the trading post.

"Now you've done it," Edison playfully scolds. "You're making us go on Indian time."

Edison rises from the chair and pushes himself down the dirt road into the trading post's gravel parking lot. Park staff have set up a shaded pavilion and chairs in front of the flat-roofed stone building raised in 1901, just as Juan Lorenzo Hubbell—that son of an American soldier and a New Mexican woman descended of an old ranching family—was feeling his roots finding the ground here. Everyone claps as Edison runs to the northeast corner of the building, where he usually parks his Toyota Tacoma pickup when he comes to work in the morning.

Wind flicks the silver-green leaves of the white poplar overhead. Edison puts his hands on his hips while the financial officer at the trading post introduces the crowd to Edison's run: that he is running to honor the survivors of the Long Walk.

The crowd of a hundred people—mostly friends and relatives—gather around Edison.

"As I make this run, I think about all the pain, the homesickness, the agony those Diné people were feeling," he says. "I'm feeling every inch of it. People talk about having a purpose. This is it, down to the core."

He holds up the black gourd rattle. "*Dilna'ííba*—Rattle. Apache made. This run, what you're seeing, is the enactment of a preparation. A little at a time, a little at a time."

He talks of how this run took forty years to prepare, how he probably ran three hundred thousand miles to get ready for it.

Recently, he ran over the mesas and dirt roads near Hilda James's territory to train for the run to Santa Fe.

"If you want to know where the blood of running comes from, here she is," Edison says as he introduces his mom.

Edison is anatomically correct. When we run, our blood talks to the world. It pulls from that heart-lung bellows and takes oxygen with hooks of hemoglobin that pass the oxygen to carriers of myoglobin (the pigment that gives our meat its red color; the more myoglobin, the darker the color). The slow-twitch muscle fibers that consume this oxygen in most people account for 50 percent of the muscles in their legs. In runners like Edison, the legs are usually 75 to 90 percent slow-twitch muscle.[20]

Some trainers believe one can measure the efficiency of these fibers by rating an athlete's VO_2 max. But many distance runners never clock inspiring VO_2 max numbers. Often, the VO_2 max is 70, where Steve Prefontaine had a VO_2 max of 84.4 and ran a 3:54 mile. Yet, Prefontaine's marathon pace was never near that of Derek Clayton or Frank Shorter.[21] Ultrarunner and biologist Berndt Heinrich believes that ultrarunners get by less on what they have and more on what they can do with it. Maybe it has to do with one's mechanical stride and position of the arms. But could one also have a *metabolic* stride? Was there a way to be efficient at the molecular level? Heinrich watched it all in a petri dish and learned that some people can have more efficient mitochondria—those energy-pulsars in our cells—than others. We each inherit these mitochondria from the egg that begins to sculpt us in the womb. From the line of our mother.

Edison greets clan relatives at the edge of the parking lot. He waves them to join the group.

Edison used his running for survival, for therapy, for the comfort. A few weeks after arriving at Haskell, several of his teammates had quit to return home. Tuckwin expected Edison to join the exodus. He could barely get the kid's name out of him. But Edison talked with his legs, his training, his running times. And Edison had other voices inside talking to him.

They spoke during a visit home during the winter break before his final semester at Haskell in 1980. He told his parents he'd planned a 135-mile run from Albuquerque to Gallup that would take him past *Tsoodził* (Bluc Bead Mountain), the sacred mountain of the South, where the bluebirds fly, where the Great Ones, the *diyin diné'é,* placed the nest with eggs of turquoise, where they secured the mountain with a knife of flint.

He didn't know why he did the run. He just needed to. His father and his younger sister, Lorraine, drove in front of him. They camped together each evening.

Edison ended his time at Haskell with a sixth-place finish at the 1980 national junior college cross-country championships. He earned All-American honors and a full scholarship to Bradley University in Peoria, Illinois. He hoped to earn a degree in fine arts as a ceramicist and to take his running to another level.

Then came the training schedule and the indoor track surfaces that have shredded many a ligament and tendon in a runner. Edison's knees started to fail. He wanted to keep them. He stopped to rest his body and mind.

He did not run for a year. He came back to school in 1985 and logged 2:26:18 at the Chicago Marathon. He decided to push himself toward the 2:20:00 qualifying time for the 1988 Olympic trials. Within the year he'd earned his bachelor of fine arts degree, found a job in a jewelry store forty miles away, and started stepping up his training.

The Boston Marathon came with strong April winds. For eighteen miles, Edison ran five-minute miles, on pace to easily qualify for the Olympic trials. Then he suffered a terrible headache that stripped him away from the lead pack. The man who'd won the marathon four times before struggled through the winds to finish at 2:18:11. Edison struggled to finish at 2:31:21.

The Olympics vanished.

He knew it was not his fastest marathon. But it felt like his bravest.

He moved back home. He worked for the Museum of Northern Arizona in Flagstaff and taught art and coached cross-country and track at an elite prep school near Prescott.

He eventually took a job at the Native American Preparatory School in Rowe, New Mexico. The school had opened in 1995 and was the nation's only privately funded intertribal college-prep school. It soon ranked among the top private schools in the nation, with nearly one hundred students from over thirty tribal nations in more than a dozen states.

Edison coached at the school and soon took on an administrative role. He was eventually promoted to headmaster, where he encountered the need to fund-raise. Nearly all the students at school depended on financial aid.

Edison said prayers over the problem. Voices spoke back to him. He would use his love of running to find the money. He performed a 208-mile run from Flagstaff to Gallup, including a hike to the top of *Dookʼoʼoosłiid* (San Francisco Peaks, the sacred mountain of the West) in six days. Do the math. That's more than thirty miles a day for nearly a week.

Edison recovered for more than a year. Then he ran ten days for 375 miles between *Sisnaajini* (Mount Blanca, the sacred mountain of the East) and *Dibé Nitsaa* (Mount Hesperus, the sacred mountain of the North). With these two runs, he raised nearly ninety thousand dollars in scholarships for his students.

During one of his runs, his dad and his sister got lost from where he was. He ran over twenty-six miles without water. Edison acknowledges that you're not supposed to be able to do that. But he did.

Edison earned something for himself that could never be money. He learned that these runs were really honoring these sacred sites. The runs became prayers. Dances. Ceremonies of survival.

We are here for a ceremony today. The Hopi have come to do an Eagle Dance. For Edison, the high end of the sensitivity for the run involves the Hopi consenting to send someone to bless the run. The Message.

Hopi runners are deeply respected by Navajo runners. And for good reason.

In the early 1900s, the trader George Wharton James would put down a dollar for a young man to run a message from Oraibi to Keam's Canyon—seventy-two miles. The runner would run out and back within thirty-six hours.[22]

Local army officers preferred Hopi runners over horses. Walter Hough saw a Hopi runner leave Oraibi at four o'clock in the afternoon and run a message to Winslow by midnight, running sixty-five miles at night over unfamiliar ground. Then the man turned around and ran home.[23]

Ganado Mucho—the chieftain for whom the town of Ganado is named—descended from the Hopi. His father was a Hopi slave who was a skilled runner. He bought his own freedom by chasing down pronghorn antelope into slot canyons, killing them, then preserving the hides for his master. The Hopi runner married into the *Tó'tsonii* clan, where his son became one of its most respected leaders.

Eduard S. Curtis—that famed "shadowcatcher"—once knew a Hopi man named Letayu, who carried a note from Keam's Canyon to Fort Wingate in two days, spending the first night at Fort Defiance. On the third morning on his return, he left Wingate before "gray dawn," got to Defiance before sunrise, and arrived at Keam's Canyon that afternoon. He'd covered over two hundred miles in three days.[24]

Charlie Talawepi was maybe thirty when he was summoned by local Indian agent Walter Runke Sr. at Tuba City. Renegades on the Navajo Reservation were causing trouble, and Runke needed to contact Flagstaff. Talawepi started out at three o'clock in the morning, alternately sprinting and jogging. Between Cameron and Gray Mountain, he saw the sun hit the San Francisco Peaks. He piled up rocks to remember how far he'd come. He was forty miles from Flagstaff at the springs near Lone Pine. He dipped piki bread into water, ate a little, got to Flagstaff at noon. He handed his message to the government official.

The San Bartholomew church once stood at the top of Second Mesa. It was built of hewn pine timbers, which the Franciscans forced Hopis to drag from the San Francisco Peaks. When the people ambushed Father Joseph de Trujillo three hundred years ago during the Pueblo Revolt, they hung him from one of those pine vigas, then burned him and used the timbers for their kiva roofs. They also threw church records and saints' effigies into the fire. When they thought the Hopi at the Pueblo of Awatovi had accepted Catholic missionaries, they trapped its people in their own kivas and burned them to death. The Hopis were not big on multiculturalism.

Famed Hopi painter Fred Kabotie created a painting in 1976 to contribute to the Bicentennial Show at the Museum of Santa Fé. Kabotie typically painted scenes of Hopi dances and gentle village life. For this composition, he painted Father Trujillo hanging in a noose and swaying from a viga. In the background, San Bartholomew church is being pulled down. A traditional bow drill is kindling a fire, a new birth of freedom for the Hopi people.

Hopi runners were also weapons of war. The best Hopi runners were sent out into Navajo country to search the enemy's *hoghans* for hair combings, saliva, and food. They would take them back to Hopi mesas and bury them as "bait." They built a fire on top of them to weaken the Navajo before an oncoming fight or war.

A Hopi man from the Horn clan once said, "Long ago when the Hopi had no sheep, no horses, no burros, they had to depend for game-capturing on their legs. They then had to cultivate their legs, think much and pray much to make them swift. Men strove in earnest to rival each other in fast running, that is why the races were run."

The runner was also a bringer of life. A Hopi man once told Alexander M. Stephen, "When the sand Chief takes the prayer feathers, to pray on them and leave them in the fields, he goes barefooted and without covering on limbs or body, that the Cloud Chiefs may see he wants rain. He runs swiftly that the clouds may come swiftly, that his prayers be quickly answered.

"He loosens his hair, and lets it hang over his shoulders, for thus the Cloud Chiefs carry the rain clouds. He makes a far circuit on the first day, because the Cloud Chiefs live far away. He goes to the northwest, southwest, northeast, and southeast, to call the attention of all the cloud chiefs … on each succeeding day, he travels in a shorter radius. It is thus we want the rain clouds to come, nearer and nearer, until on the concluding day of the ceremony they shall have come overhead and poured down the heavy rain upon ourselves, our houses and all the surrounding lands, and we may see the arroyo full of running water and listen to its sweet sound."

This is labeled by anthropologists as *sympathetic magic*.

Ruben Saufkie Sr. wears a linen shirt with red and turquoise beadwork stitched into the shoulders. He and his son have come today from Second Mesa to give a Hopi eagle dance for the ceremony of Edison's run.

Ruben carries a simple hand drum. His son wears a set of eagle wings over each arm. A cap of eagle feathers covers his head and hides his eyes. The crowd gathers around them under the cottonwoods in the parking lot.

"We are all here," Ruben says, "with our ancestors."

He speaks of how the Hopi did a run from Polacca (the farthest western mesa) to Mexico City. They did the run to honor water and protest the mines of Peabody Coal.

"They have wasted so many gallons of our precious water," Ruben says. "Without water, we will not survive. We need to come together. Ivan Gamble was a Navajo man who did this run with us. He is no longer with us now. He is with the ancestors. Our creator made this world and appointed us guardians of this world. We were never to possess it. Since we are here, we are the ones who can make things right for the rest of humanity and for all life. Hear this, while we dance for you."

Ruben starts on the hand drum.

His son, Ruben Saufkie Jr., postures as an eagle leaping into the air and spreads the wings. His feet find the drum and his crouch makes his body an eagle in the wind. You have to look carefully beneath the feathers to find his arm tattoo that reads "Sacrifice" in that cursive kind of writing one sees inked across the arms of many a cholo cruising the streets of Española, New Mexico. His left ear is pierced. Another tattoo bands his wrist. A half-moon is tattooed on his palm. He's spent time off the mesa.

During a series of hops, the cap of eagle feathers falls from his head. Edison walks up and retrieves it for him.

Saufkie ends the drum. Someone points to the sky. The clouds over the trading post shift into the shape of an eagle. This happens.

"This last song is a prayer for all humanity," Saufkie says. "So we can grow with the seeds we've planted. We must put aside our petty differences. So the rains can fall and feed us all. Find compassion within to forgive ourselves. This is the only way to peace. This is the message."

Forty-four people stand in the shade of the Siberian elm. There's a lot to forgive.

"And if your hearts are moved," Ruben says, "I will set this basket on the ground so that you can offer what you wish, so that way my son here can buy dinner for his girlfriend at Burger King."

Everyone laughs there. And the dance happens and money falls into the basket.

Ruben says the eagle feathers on the wings danced by his son were blessed by the Dalai Lama on his eightieth birthday. So the dancer will move around and give a blessing to everyone. Edison steps forward and holds out his hands, palms up. The dancer flaps the wings over Edison's head, shoulders, hands, and legs. Edison pours water on the ground after the dancer leaves him. Then the eagle dancer blesses Edison's family. Then the rest of us.

It is difficult to describe all the forces that lift tons of water into the sky and roll them through veils of ice and wind and dust to make the ice pellets that become rain clouds. But these are the forces that fist up my spine when the eagle feathers go around my head and neck and hands. It is something.

Now the crowd breaks up. Some head for the tables of food. It is a simple affair. Chili, chips, salsa, cookies, watermelon, cakes, and fruit punch.

Edison introduces a local Diné rock band set to play for the crowd, fronted by Damon John. The name of the band is Deja Voo. Edison says they should call themselves "Navajo Jahn."

Edison speaks with a reporter from the *Navajo Times*. She asks why he is doing this run. He says, "It has nothing to do with running, it has nothing to do with athleticism. I believe in what was said. There is a comfort in what I'm doing. There's rugs involved. Spider Woman is involved. The Emergence is involved. The language is involved. And the thinking process is involved."[25]

Then Edison leaves with Lorraine and Jason to rest.

Deja Voo plays their first number: "Cocaine" by Eric Clapton.

The eagle wings have been folded and placed away in whatever box keeps them pristine.

There is a lot to forgive.

In the *Dził nahadili ch'oshgai'* (Chuska Mountains) the Diné and the Ute make war medicine together. They ride against the Comanche, a tribe who sent chiefs to Santa Fé and openly declared they would wipe the Diné off the earth. They ride for days and hit a Comanche camp while the warriors are away hunting buffalo. The Diné hunt the Comanche and destroy the camp. The Comanche come back and turn a Ute camp to ashes and smoldering hides.

The Spanish fear they may be wiped out by the reprisals between Navajo and Comanche. But they manage to avoid each other in cycles of raiding, theft, and murder. The Navajo hunt buffalo and burn the tipis they find. The Comanche roam and take whatever corn they want from Navajo fields. In that same year, the British colonies on the other side of the grass ocean powder the skin of a resurrected corpse they call "the Republic" and ask a dead world to live again in a new nation conceived in Liberty called "The United States of America."

By 1804, the Diné ask the Spanish to leave the missions at Cubero and Encinal by April. They see they are building them into the military forts the Diné often raid along the Río Grande. The Spanish will not leave.

One night in the spring, more than two hundred Navajo men ride into the plaza of Cubero. They smash into houses and drive off cattle and horses. They leave the villagers with nightmares.

By the middle of the summer, the villagers learn that the high stone walls are worthless against the Navajo warriors. They find a cave three miles north of the village and start to hide in it when the Diné war parties ride in. A thousand warriors storm the village soon after.

It will be war to the knife for the next sixty years.

To hold these Christian forts, the Spanish governor requests troops out of Mexico. Lt. Antonio Narbona rides up from Sonora with a large force in the winter of 1805. They move out to Canyon de Chelly, where the petroglyphs sit on the wall.

Matt Hannifin builds toys. Some spin and display the properties of gravity. Some whir and emit tendrils of electricity to reveal the forces surrounding us all the time that we never see.

He used these toys as a science teacher in classrooms in Switzerland, France, and Spain. He opened a science toy store in Santa Fe. Then he sold it and moved to Colorado, where he opened another store. Now he travels anywhere from Wisconsin to Ireland with his company Science Toy Magic, LLC, and gives science presentations in eleven languages. He will show up at a school and give a fifty-minute demonstration on the principles of physics. If you book him for the whole day, you get a reduced rate. He will present in Spanish, French, Swedish, Italian, Irish (Gaelic), Mandarin Chinese, German, Hawai'ian, and Warlpiri. Right now he is working on his Navajo.

Edison was the first to teach him Navajo. Matt has just practiced a greeting he has spoken to Edison. He has written it out in a notebook. He shows me the tally marks above the phrase he has written in red pen that testify to how he has practiced the phrase over three hundred times.

Matt wears a faded gray baseball cap, jeans, and worn shoes. His gray polo shirt looks like he just bought it today. It is over ten years old. Embroidered over the heart is a symbol of a hoop with four eagle feathers hanging down. In the center of the hoop burns that traditional Greek torch, the fire of knowledge blazing. The text below reads, "Native American Prep School."

He has read my other books while living in Australia for two years. He took in the culture. He has dual-citizenship there. He speculates that he probably is 2 percent Australian. He also speculates that I am over 30 percent Navajo.

I ask him about Edison, who was his boss at the Native American Prep school.

"How would I describe him? How should I phrase it? Let me put it this way. I am a simple man. I'm like a balloon. You take the surface of a balloon, and that's what's there. I'm a very superficial person. Really. I'm just aware of it. For example, I have a tough time doing things that I would consider wrong. People have sometimes complimented me on it. 'Wow, you're just such a moral person,' they'll say. But it's not that. I'm just superficial. I don't even wrestle with moral questions. I would just never go against the programming I received from my family growing up. I just . . . I can't. My wife? She's like an onion. She's got layers and layers of who she is. But me? *Balloon.* Knowing Edison? It's like . . . what do you say about Gandhi? Imagine you worked with Gandhi, that you joked with him, laughed with him. Not just the iconic figure of Gandhi. But the man. So I had that experience at our school. And whatever understanding I have about things on this level."

He lays a hand flat against his chest to demonstrate a plane of thinking. He places his other flat hand above his head.

"Edison is on this level. He understands something I do not. And we're probably going to die that way."

He laughs as though discovering his own joke for the first time. "And with Edison as the dean of students, everything was done with dignity and honor. It was just amazing. We sent kids to Harvard, Yale, to MIT. And they were *ready*. We had a coach who was an English teacher and an author, so there was never any question about which was better, athletics or academics. I mean, your academics is first. No question. It's not even a debate. And that's a good feeling to not have to worry about that. We had students and we did amazing things with them. If that's all Edison had ever done, it would have been an amazing achievement in and of itself. And when I think back on it, I've taught physics in France, Switzerland, Australia. But I think the work I did at the Native American Prep School was the finest work I ever did. I really do believe that."

But the dream came to an end. The school functioned by adhering to four fundamental concepts: culture, character, community, and career.

Edison taught using the circle. The circle flows like the red rainbow around the Navajo basket, that path between the mountains and the clouds. There is birth, adolescence, adulthood, and old age. In that circle, one finds the balance, the ability to conquer things, to obtain that college degree or to have that career.

They kept the boys and girls separate in the dorms. These things were changed by the new management. The mortal wound came with the logical fallacy that academic achievement cures social ills or can somehow mitigate them. With the admission of students with social problems who had been kicked out of other schools, it became almost impossible for the school to function.

"I love those students, too," Matt says. "I want to help those students. But that school was not the place for them. They can work out those problems. There are ways to do that. But not in an academically rigorous setting. So I was asked to change grades, to raise grades. And I would not. So I was given my walking papers. Now I'm sure those foundations with money were just circling that school. They were just ready to unload money to us. Now I want you to imagine that I'm the Bill and Melinda Gates Foundation. And I show up with my big fat checkbook.

And I'm about to sign over some serious cash. But, ah, I start hearing things from universities, about these kids showing up, unprepared. And now I take my big fat checkbook and now I put that away."

It is summer when Don Lorenzo Gutiérrez joins up with nearly three hundred Mexicans who ride west for two hundred miles across the pale plains of badlands chalk and over the pine and aspens of the Chuska Mountains. They trot up Canyon de Chelly, firing and killing as they can.

Navajo warriors stand and fire arrows at the Spanish. The Spanish kill them with their muskets. The children run. The Mexicans shoot them if they look like they might be old enough to fight them. The mothers and grandmothers lead the children up into cliff hideouts away from the Mexicans.

An old woman in one of the large caves yells and spits in Spanish at the invaders. She does not care that she reveals their location. She believes they are out of range and does not understand the killing powers of the musket. The Spanish militia shoot up into the cave and the ricochets fly down on people huddled on their knees. The shelter becomes a house of corpses. The militia fires more than two hundred bullets. These bullet marks are still on the roof of the cave today.

Some call this place Massacre Cave. Many local people call this place *Adah Aho' doo' nili* because when the first New Mexico militia man climbed up to the cave to sort through the dead bodies of the people who'd been killed by the volleys of bullets and ricochets, a woman emerged from the corpses and stood in front of him. She grabbed him, wrestled him away from the cave, and the two fell in a death-clutch from the cliff. *Adah Aho' doo' nili* means The Place Where Two Fell Off.

The militiamen stand over the dead bodies of the Diné warriors. Then they stoop with knives and cut off their ears. They tie up twenty-four women and children to ride back to the slave market in Santa Fé. The women cover their children's eyes when the militia men run the forty-two ears on a string and swing it as a trophy. The Mexican governor in Santa Fé will pay them bounty for these kills. The ears are good as money.

41

The Hopi Eagle Dance at Hubbell Trading Post. Ganado, Arizona.
Photo by Jason Bunion.

Don Lorenzo Gutiérrez takes some of this money and builds himself a thriving ranching operation in Pajarito. His son's daughter will marry a soldier from a place called the United States of America. They will have children. One son will be named Juan Lorenzo, for his great-grandfather. He will establish a trading post in Ganado in his early thirties under the name Juan Lorenzo Hubbell. Hubbell Trading Post.

With this violation of the sacred ground of Canyon de Chelly, the Diné feel their world becoming something else. Their warriors fall to ghosts of lead whistling through the air. Their ears become coin. The women feel ropes tighten over their wrists as they are walked to the east, to *Nleidi Akee Bitah,* the land of the *Nakai.* The woman stands at the edge of the cave. She grabs the murderer of her family and assures his death with her own. What was this woman's name? Who did she love? What did she lose? Where is she now?

She is running. She is running with Edison.

⊹ DAY FOUR

A morning breeze stirs the green cottonwoods growing along the Pueblo Colorado Wash. The execution of the tamarisk we saw at Chinle has also been carried out in Ganado. Willows and tall grass grow along the meandering stream that had once gullied twelve feet deep into the sand between the armored banks of tamarisk. Those days are gone and greener days are here.

A large mound of earth stands across the road from where Edison will take his first strides. Some notice the strangeness of a mound of earth fenced in with barbed wire. This is the Wide Reeds House, that place where Anasazi people had settled along the wash. Archaeologists had excavated the ruin and found shell necklaces, woven baskets, corn stored in jars for the people who would be returning someday but who never did. They found arrowheads knapped from pieces of petrified wood. They examined the seeds and pollen grains in the house and found no evidence of sagebrush growing in the area. Now it is everywhere. Those days are gone.

Pencil drawing of Edison Eskeets
when he ran for Haskell. Pencil
drawing by Keanan Eskeets.

In the summer of 1816, a massive Comanche war party moves through Spanish territory with the governor's quiet permission. Its destination is the southern slopes of *Tsoodził* (Blue Bead Mountain). The Comanches attack the Navajo rancherías. They torture who they do not kill. The Navajos consider abandoning the land. And they do. Thirty years later, very few remain unless they are allied with the Spanish.

The Spanish graze their cattle on the grass growing in patches between the basalt and sagebrush of Diné land. The Navajo steal the cattle. These raids are—in Diné logic—merely reclaiming their grass that has passed into the stomachs of the cattle. They often steal the cowherds and take them into the tribe. It is a world where numbers matter. There is nothing yet known as an 'arms race.' But there is always a race to see who will have the superior numbers.

Edison begins the dance. He runs up to the turn off at Ganado Lake and the water shines the blue reflection of the white clouds. I attended my first Blessingway ceremony at a *hoghan* near that lake. The man who lived there, Alvin Begay, had run with Edison at Haskell and had won championships. He was the man who taught me the ceremonial names for birds and how to signal *atsa'* (eagle) when it flies overhead. This way, you receive the blessing of the wings of the eagle.

That man's daughter, Alvina Begay, became a champion runner and nearly qualified for the Olympics. She is still sponsored by Nike, has coached for Wings of America, and promotes running across the Reservation. In 2017, she posted a 2:44:05 time at the Boston Marathon.

This is a land of runners.

The land rolls up in elevation to the east, with the sagebrush plains rising to forest of piñon and juniper and then crowns of *ndishchii* (ponderosa pine). We stop after six miles and Edison rests in the camping chair. He asks for his Sobé water and Jay-Lynn can't find it.

"This is where I have my diva moment," Edison jokes. "'What!? What do you mean?! Darn it! Darn it!'" He gets up and feigns slamming his chair into the road and laughs at himself.

"*Mą'ii'. Mą'ii',*" he whispers.

In Navajo, this word often means "Coyote." But it also indicates a behavior that is troublemaking. Drama queen. This is one of the four fundamental laws I was taught growing up with my Diné step-dad, who is also a champion runner, having held the Arizona state championship cross-country record time for several years. He ran for Pima Community College and qualified to attend the Olympic trials. He did not have the money, so he couldn't go. It happens to many Native runners.

The fundamental laws are simple. You are taught *ana'haat'i*—Don't gossip about people. You are taught *o'chííd'i*—Don't put people down and make them feel less. They say *ill'í*—Don't be petty or defiant for no reason. They say *tse'ch'í*—Don't whine or overdramatize things. Edison knows these phrases and lives them.

We stop along the road. The wild flax coils to the sky in blues and purples. Shards of petrified wood shine in the clay earth.

Edison lets the wind cool the sweat in his gray hair. At the trading post, Edison says they have many coyotes (he pronounces the name *kai-oats)*. When they cross the road, the old men at the post won't leave. They just wait. Then someone else will drive out ahead of them. Usually it's a driver with an out-of-state plate.

Coyotes are powerful.

Sixteen *naat'áanii* (chieftains) ride through the pines and oaks, trot their horses over the powdery basins of the Río Puerco, and arrive at Jémez. They are journeying to Santa Fé to make peace talks with the governor. This breaks an unspoken rule. They request the commander of the fort allow them to pass to Santa Fé to meet the governor. The commander invites the chiefs inside.

The commander invites them to sit in a circle and he smokes tobacco with them from a long clay pipe. He makes show of friendship. A Mexican sits on either side of a *naat'áanii*. The commander gives a signal. The Mexicans on either side grab the chieftains by the arms. Men run out with knives and stab the Navajos in the heart. The Mexicans throw the dead bodies over the wall and cover them with dirt in a ditch.

A few days later, five Navajo men ride down to the Jémez River and ask about their chieftains. The Mexicans say the *naat'áanii* rode on to Santa Fé. They invite them to come over. They cross. They sit in the circle to smoke tobacco. The Mexicans sit next to them on either arm. The knives come out. The ditch is fed.

A day passes. Three men appear. They ask. They are invited into the smoking circle. The ditch eats.

A few days later, two more appear. These Navajos are invited to the smoking circle. But something is on the wind. They will not cross the Jémez River. Some Mexicans ride down on them. The Navajos get to their horses and they are gone.

This story comes from General Thomas James, an American trader at Jémez. He meets a Mexican who helped stab the Navajos. He shows James his knife. The Mexican shakes it and says it killed eight of them. James calls it cold-blooded murder.

It is said that to become a *naat'áanii,* a man had to emerge through trials on the war trail and the making of peace. He would need to kill enemies and show the depth of his rage by scalping and then chewing on the bloody scalp like a piece of leather. He would need to show he could love children. He often held slaves who he would gradually make into his family. He was a mentor.

Some would prove themselves with a coming-of-age ritual that took as long as it took. The man stripped to his loincloth and strapped on his best running moccasins. Taking only a bag of *tádídíín* (sacred corn pollen) and a knife, the man went out alone and ran down, trapped, or captured a coyote. He had to take the *tádídíín* from the bag and put it on the coyote's paws, sift it through the skin and hair, pick the corn pollen up and collect it back into the bag, and then release the coyote unharmed. That *tádídíín* then became a powerful medicine for him for the rest of his life.

Coyotes are powerful.

This practice was abandoned because it was too difficult. The kind of men who could do it seemed to end up being murdered as they fought to defend their ground.

Who were these twenty-four *naat'áanii* who stepped into that smoking circle? What training had they endured? What marriages had they decided? What crops did they plant? What horses had they tamed? Where had they hunted deer? What vengeances had they taken? What doom had they sensed?

All ran in the morning. Their bodies went into a ditch. The rattle shakes.

All ran like Edison. They are running with him now.

Edison runs the easy rolling rise from the seven thousand–foot sage-brush plain, through the piñon forest, to the eight thousand–foot elevation of the Defiance Plateau. He strides between shadows cast by ponderosa pines. Joe Lunny rides behind him on a bicycle. Joe wears a neon-green vest to warn oncoming traffic of Edison's presence. Joe protects Edison with his body. The cool ground assures Edison will stay hydrated.

"The Great Ones are here," he says. "The goodness is here."

Joe Lunny rides behind Edison on the Defiance Plateau.
Photo by Jay-Lynn Bunion.

Running down to *Tséhootsooʼí* (The Meadow Between The Rocks).
St. Michaels, Arizona. Photo by Jay-Lynn Bunion.

That dawn, he runs from the 8,000-foot Defiance Summit to the 6,800-foot *Tséhootsooʼí* valley. When he hits the base of the Summit, everything changes. He feels the thrust.

"It was understood there," he says. "It was understood by the people that a great change was going to take place. It's like when you're riding a bike and the handlebars get pulled sideways and you totally wipe out. You get the wind knocked out of you. You're moaning for a good five minutes or so. The definite change is there."

The two men make it back to their band from Jémez. Someone sends a runner.

The runner spreads the word of the fallen *naatʼáanii* at Jémez.

The Navajos sing many war songs, some caught in ink by various ethnographers. The men sang them and transformed into *shash*—the black bear who comes down like a storm of vengeance from the mountains. One song goes:

Big black bear.
My moccasins are black obsidian.
My leggings are black obsidian.
My shirt is black obsidian.
I am girdled with a gray arrowsnake.
Black snakes project from my head.
With zigzag lightning projecting from the ends of my feet I step.
With zigzag lightning streaming out from my knees I step.
With zigzag lightning
streaming out from the tips of my fingers I work my hands.
With zigzag lightning streaming out from the tip of my tongue I speak.
Now a disc of pollen rests on the crown of my head.
Gray arrowsnakes and rattlesnakes eat it.
Black obsidian and zigzag lightning streams out from me in four ways.
Where they strike the earth, bad things and bad talk.
It causes the arrows to spread out.
Long life, something frightening I am.
Now I am.[26]

The men take this song when the two men spread the word from Jémez back to the tribe. The men take this song to seek the bottom of their vengeance. It is hard to find. They search for it in Valverde, Las Huertas, Estancia, Santa Fé. They kill the men and they kill the women and children. They put everything to fire. They ride their horses. Eagle feathers flail from their caps made of mountain lion scalps and bear skin. They burn down the country around the town of Taos. Then they disappear.

General Thomas James is asked to lead an expedition against them. He declines and prefers to be "a spectator in such a war."[27]

The governor funds a massive expedition against the Navajos. They capture only a Navajo man too old to run.

Six months earlier, Edison had visited Fort Defiance in autumn, to say prayers at the site.

"I wanted the run to have that connection to that place," he says. "It was important to say, 'I was there,' and not just look at it from a distance and wave at it."

Then he turned and ran along the paved road past the fields that had once grown *naadą́ą́'* (corn) and *ch'ee jii'aan* (melons) and *nazísí* (squash) from the waters of Black Creek. Today, the bare, sandy fields are haunted by sprawls of Russian knapweed and spines of tumbleweed. Every year, the men who own these fields go out and plow them with their tractors like their fathers and grandfathers had done. They are expecting something. But it does not come.

An Anglo friend of mine who worked on the Reservation for twenty years once had a conversation with a tribal council member who told him he couldn't wait to have the fields around Black Creek planted and sown with crops. The land was lying fallow, he said, and it had all that nutrient inside waiting to just burst out and grow things.

He did not know that "lying fallow" would mean that farmers were growing grass and other nitrogen-fixing plants on the land and leaving it to recharge the soil. Instead, people let their livestock graze it until the plants had all died and erosion finished the execution.

By summer, Navajo warriors have hit Tomé, Laguna, Belén, Albuquerque, and crossed the southern Rockies to strike Mora in the far east. By the fall of 1822, the governor sends out peace emissaries. There is no historical evidence to show that the Navajo murder them.

The new governor, José Antonio Vizcarra, has a vision for the Navajos. He says they should all be baptized and settle down into pueblos that the Spanish might more easily control. The Navajo chieftains ask for their women and children back. Vizcarra says they've been baptized and can't be returned. The war continues. Navajos kill six at Socorro, then eight Mexicans at Sabinal.

Vizcarra sets out on a three-month campaign to Canyon de Chelly that summer. They kill fifteen men and capture thirty-six women and children. The Navajos follow them back and attack the outskirts of Santa Fé.

The Diné children are made into slaves. By November, seventy-one of them have been baptized. The Church describes them as "purchased," "sold," or "ransomed." They usually sell for a hundred pesos.

Edison crosses the New Mexico border at Tse Bonito, New Mexico.
Photo by Jay-Lynn Bunion.

At the traffic light in Window Rock, in sight of the New Mexico border, three men meet Edison at the corner. They wear business slacks and collared shirts. Their hair is cropped short and gelled. They look like they work in a bank. They do work in a bank, in the Wells Fargo just up the road. They heard about the run and the tallest man claims to be a medicine man. He offers Edison a plastic cup of water as a blessing. It is hard for Edison to see their expressions. The three men wear sunglasses. He obliges them and drinks. He shakes their hands. Then he shakes the rattle and keeps running.

He crosses the New Mexico border in Tse Bonito, New Mexico. That evening, Edison finishes the run at the Speedy's gas station at Black Hat.

Edison steps out of the Armada in the cool air. He takes the first two miles with no pause in his step.

"The feeling today is hope," he says. "I think when people were moving. People are just being moved. There's a lot of uncertainty. And a lot of hope. I feel that. All the way into Gallup, man. All the way into Gallup."

Edison runs into Gallup and the city opens before him. The grounds for the Gallup Flea Market—"the place to see and be seen," the locals joke—lie to the east. It is a place where one can buy guns, horseshoes, comic books, yoga mats, dreamcatchers, frybread, and wolf-hybrid puppies on any given Saturday. Alfalfa hay is fairly priced and you get a snow cone before you leave, even in the winter.

The town had flowed out from the tentacles of the Atlantic and Pacific Railroad. It was named Gallup by 1881, when it became a headquarters for the construction of the southern transcontinental rail route. The town's name comes from the paymaster for the railroad, named David L. Gallup.

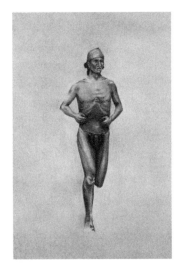

A Navajo runner competes in a footrace in Gallup, New Mexico, on July 4, 1905. Photo by Simion Shemberger and donated by Dave and Judy Woolsey. Pencil drawing by Keanan Eskeets

Some call it a violent town. In some years, Gallup had a violent crime rate nearly five times the national average and the highest rate in New Mexico.

In Gallup, Edison sees the changes while he sips water.

"The ever-changing society," he says. "The Age of Industry. Changes are evident. The pace of living. It is slow. Way better than the East Coast. But you have a sense that people are in a hurry. When I was in school, it was different. You just made your way. You had your lunch. And you go home. Then, kids were enjoying their school days. Now, they call it their educational experience. Or their high school career. It's like, 'By the weekend, I'll be in college.'"

He chuckles and runs another two miles.

The chieftain Narbona feels the shock of the stolen children. So do the Mexicans. They do not travel in force to *Diné Bikéyah*. There is not a record of a Mexican killed by a Navajo. Still the children disappear from Navajo country. They emerge in wisps of ink in Catholic churches. One hundred and fifty appear there in the year of 1826. Then the window closes and we see them no more.

The Mexicans savor the slaves. Their roses grow easier around the haciendas. Fewer weeds appear in the fields. The cows get milked and pastured and watered. More people migrate north in the borders of the now-independent republic of Mexico.

Edison soaks the red bandana and drips water from the bottle over his head.

"In the old ways, the *hoghan* is actually not a house. *Ho-ghan*. That's the landscape. The *hoghan*. The shelter was just a place to sleep. It was the land that was actually your home."

He points to where the traffic and roads condense to the central iron tracks of the railroad running through Gallup's center.

"All peoples. Zuni. Navajo. Pueblo. Hopi," he says. "It was a place. It became home. They created this little town for themselves. The location is chiseled out. The land is created in such a way that is emotionally comforting. So that emotional aspect is conquered. Now you lay down that railroad track. Those cottonwoods. The trading post. It was to further their way of living. We made it a place."

The Mexicans hunt for more slaves at Abiquiú, Cubero, Cebolleta, Sandía, Jémez, and Cochití. An expedition of a thousand Mexicans crosses the desert in the winter of 1835.

The thousand Mexican militiamen and Jémez warriors wind up the flanks of the Chuska Mountains. The desert they have crossed extends in a gray dream to the east. They do not see the two hundred Navajo warriors waiting in the scrub oaks and in the dark firs. One cups his hands and hoots like an owl. The Navajos loose their arrows. They roll logs down on the Mexicans and trap their horses. Less than a dozen men escape.

They walk Salvador, the war captain of the Jémez, to the edge of a cliff and force him to jump to his death. The Mexican survivors return knowing that Narbona choreographed this death act in this mountain corridor that will become known as Narbona Pass. Once the Navajos have left the corpses for the crows, they have an *N'dah*—an Enemy Way ceremony—to purify their bodies of the ghosts of the men they have killed.

That was the end of many people.

From Taos, people begin chanting a song along the Río Grande in Spanish:

> *If you are in combat*
> *And your troop did not win,*
> *Ask God to rescue you*
> *If your enemy is Navajo.*
>
> *When you go to Navajo land*
> *Prepare for mortal trouble*
> *Because death awaits there,*
> *Firm and without compromise.*[28]

By the end of that summer, the Mexicans ask for peace. Their

Lorraine hands water mid-stride to Edison. Photo by Jason Bunion.

demands are absurd. Then they break the peace when Don José Chaves leads fifty young men out to strike it rich by stealing and selling Navajo bodies.

You could sell a Navajo woman in the plaza at Santa Fé or Taos and get five hundred pesos. You get the same if you sell her children.

Edison runs past Fire Rock Casino. Each night, the parking lot is full. Gambling was a part of the old ways, a way of entertainment. But Edison knows that the spear-throwing, horse-racing, arrow-shooting, card-playing games of the Diné are not the same as the computerized slot machines and video poker games people tap and play while quaffing cheap alcohol.

The day's run ends at Iyanbito. Edison claps for Jason, Lorraine, and Jay-Lynn. He knows they are running with him.

That morning, National Public Radio announces that a storm chaser from Missouri has died. He had his ashes thrown into the thrum of the cyclone. He did this because he thought it "would be fun."

Film producer Harvey Weinstein—who helped finance films such as *Jane Eyre* and *Shakespeare in Love*—appears in court in New York City under charges that he forced oral sex from a woman and raped another.

A group of Mexicans at the border throws rocks at border-patrol agents. One of the officers pulls his pistol and shoots a Mexican woman in the face.

Edison is running east. He follows Route 40 until the turnoff for Route 66 at Continental Divide. From here, all water flows east to the Atlantic. He points to a roadside from where we start.

"That spot right there," he says. "That's halfway."

Edison felt this first. He was driving back to his home near Santa Fe,

Running toward Continental Divide. Photo by Jay-Lynn Bunion.

and he thought, "This is it. The halfway point." And then he marked it on the odometer. He was off by less than three miles.

"Billy Mills was like that," Edison says. "In the Olympics, he was totally discounted among the other runners. It was 1964 and he was running the 10,000 meters. Some low-level newscaster asked him about the outcome of the race. And he said, 'Well, the winning time will be 28:24.' And he was off by one second. *One second.* He was just so well-trained. You run those laps, hit those turns, where your one arm does the pumping. You don't let that other arm go. You're just wasting energy. He was so tuned into that."

Mills had attended Haskell fifteen years before Edison. He emerged from the Lakota nation, went on to run for the University of Kansas, won the individual title at the 1960 national cross-country championships, and joined the marines after he graduated. He continued his training for the Olympics while in the Marine Reserve and competed as First Lieutenant Billy Mills in the 10,000-meter race. That's twenty-five laps around the track, about 6.2 miles. In the race in Tokyo, Mills was not favored at all. His Olympic trial time was not within a minute of the Australian Ron Clarke, the world-record holder in the 10,000 meters. Clarke had once run that distance in 28:15. That's running a 4:55 mile for six miles.

Mills kept up with the pack of runners at the lead. In the last two laps, the pack was lapping other runners. Mills told the story of the last two laps at my intermediate school in Ganado, twenty-six years ago, while we all sat on the wooden basketball court in the Ganado Middle School field house.

Mills said that in the last lap he passed a German runner and the runner had an eagle on his jersey. Mills thought about his father, about the strength of the sky. He chanted to himself. I can win. Wings of an eagle. I can win. Wings of an eagle. I won. I won. I won. I won. Mills told us he heard that phrase—"wings of an eagle"—in his head a thousand times in just thirty yards. Time and space became fantasies.

And then he feels the tape break across his chest.

It's considered one of the greatest upsets in Olympic history.

Mills went to find the German runner after the race to tell him that the eagle on his jersey had helped him win. He found the man and went to shake his hand. There was no eagle on the jersey. It was his perception. Some might call this "a vision." When you run, you see them.

Edison crests the hill and looks out to the country I've often called *Dootł'izhii Dził bitah'íí* (Blue Mountain Country).

We take to the quieter, slower pace of Route 66 running alongside Route 40. Screams of steel and glass cut the air. The crickets sing loud through the screams in the grass along the highway barrier.

To the north, red mesas lift to the sky. The plains of sagebrush, white clay, and thin grass open to the east. Spreads of grama grass, bulrush, and cattails emerge from wherever water finds a low spot in the land. To the south, the heads of the Zuni mountains rise in dark piñon and ponderosa pine.

"I'm really feeling the elevation," Edison says. "Wow. It's a beautiful landscape, though. It's beautiful. But it's brutal."

They are almost the same word in this country.

He is sitting after the last two miles. *Tsoodził* looms before us in pyramids of blue and green shadow.

I ask what he thinks when he sees that mountain. Edison says he thinks of words. Songs. Ceremonies. He says it's a fair question, but I know he's not ready to answer it. He runs.

Cebolleta Mesa rises dark and jagged through a haze of heat at the base of *Tsoodził.* Beyond lie the lands of Chaco Canyon and the stories so old they are lost in sand.

The party of Mexicans passes from Cebolleta to the Río Chaco. They are hunting flesh. They see no Navajos. They ride beneath a sandstone cliff. Narbona again conducts the fight. The Navajo warriors shoot from ambush. They spring down in their caps of lynx scalps and mountain lion hides. They club the Mexicans at the back of their skulls and kill them, the way they have seen mountain lions kill deer. The warriors believe they are lions.

Only two boys survive. One is Manuel Antonio Chávez, the sixteen-year-old brother of the expedition's leader. He has seven arrows in his body. One arrow passes completely through his torso. The other is a Navajo boy who has been raised among Chávez's family and has come with them to hunt for Navajo slaves.

Narbona and his men do not leave the ambush site until they have killed all the slavers. Chávez hides. He hunts along the canyon until he finds his brother's body. He and the Navajo boy bury it. What words travel between them? What dreams did they have? What did they say? What did they not say?

They walk for two days to a spring the Spanish call Ojo del Oso. The Navajo call it *Shash Bitó* (Bear Springs). The Navajo boy dies of his wounds. Chávez walks another two days to the mission at Cebolleta. He lives. He will be at Bear Springs some years later.

Chávez goes on to travel to St. Louis, New Orleans, New York. He crosses the ocean to the island of Cuba. But he returns to the work of his family: herding sheep and hunting slaves. He becomes a respected captain of militia, earns a reputation as a tough fighter and a killer of Navajos. His people nickname him *Leoncito*. Little Lion.[29]

A year later, three more war parties go into Navajo country. They kill nearly twenty. A month later, Navajos attack Albuquerque. They kill five people.

In December of 1840, the Navajo give sixteen men to the coffins of Belén.

The Americans come into the country. They appoint a headman from the region of *Dootł'izhii Dził bitah'íí* (Blue Mountain Country) as their liaison with the Diné, a man the Spanish call Sandoval. Sandoval does not have it easy. He is a border dweller. On the east, Mexicans harass him and push his pastures. Sometimes Comanche will ride up and threaten extermination.

On the west are his own people. Their young men leave their country to make war on the Mexicans, to win cattle, sheep, and a name. When the Mexicans send out expeditions of revenge, Sandoval's people are on the border and are the low-hanging fruit. So Sandoval does a deal with the Mexicans. He speaks Spanish. When the Americans come to see him for the first time around *Tsoodził*, the turquoise mountain, he has just returned from a trip. He was hunting women and children to sell into slavery. The women and children are Navajos.

After two miles, Edison sits.

"I've really been needing quiet time lately," he says. He confesses he was even annoyed by a prairie dog that ran alongside him for fifty yards that morning. "I need just quiet time to recover from the experience. It's strange. I've never needed that before. I think it's the age. But I'm also feeling a lot. A lot. There are burial grounds all along here. This is where they would have walked. They were traveling over there. The children wouldn't make it. The grandparents couldn't make it. The parents would dig a little grave. They'd say, 'We put you in there. We've tucked you in. Be well.'"

I ask what he feels now.

"Voices. Words. But the feeling is . . . 'It's better. Now. Now it's coming well. It's better.'"

Edison stands up and shakes the rattle. He runs ahead.

Lorraine shakes her head. "He's a real Navajo philosopher. A self-made philosopher. He'll say things or he'd tell me things and I'd think, 'Where does that thinking even *come from,* Ed?' He's like a revitalized Bruce Lee. He'll just say the word, 'Water.' Just water. And he can talk about just that for hours and be totally focused on how it connects to people, to you, to everything. So that's why I tell him, 'You're just a self-made philosopher.'"

Portrait of the Diné chieftain Narbona. Sketch by R. H. Karn.

Edison begins outside Thoreau, New Mexico, population 1,400 people. The chapter house for Thoreau sits near the base of salmon-red sandstone cliffs that seem illuminated from within against the blue sky. Grama grass taps chain-link fencing along the main road. Thoreau is known as the home of Ben Shelly, once Navajo Nation President. It is also known for suicides.

Fifteen teenagers and young adults killed themselves between late 2009 and 2010. A Teach for America volunteer in the community decided to raise money to buy an old building and create a community center painted in bright colors. Kids could meet with counselors, browse the internet, and eat popcorn and peanut butter sandwiches. Brochures on STDs and college counseling stood in metal baskets.

The town's name is properly pronounced "Thah-Roo." It was named for an army postmaster with the last name "Theroux." The Navajo name

Tsoodził (The Blue Mountain). Mount Taylor. Photo by Jason Bunion.

for the place, *Dl'oo Yazhi* (Little Prairie Dog), comes from the short Anglo trader who used to scamper between the counter and his warehouse to bring the fruits of American capitalism in exchange for wool and rugs.

Edison shows up in black Nike shorts, green Nike shirt, and gray and green Avia shoes. He wears the same ripstop fabric hat. He walks quietly into a run. He will dance ten miles today. In the first half-mile, I follow while Lorraine, Jason, and Jay-Lynn are still prepping. Edison seems almost antsy to move or like he hasn't slept fully. He taped his feet early that morning. Now he is running. In less than half a mile, he stoops mid-stride and picks up a chunky piece of metal. He hands it off to me through the window.

"I'll keep this for my work," he says.

It is a mason's chisel. I stow it for Edison down the road. Jason pulls around us. Edison dances four miles and walks to the Armada.

We pass *Tsé Chii'ii* (Red Rocks), spanning against the blue sky. Here is where Edison met his first teachers. The sheep.

Edison met the sheep out there, herding on the first mesa and then the top mesa. His mom can still hear the train on the other side of the mountain.

He and I discussed this over cups of coffee in the warehouse of Hubbell Trading Post in the winter before the run. We sat in our winter coats across from each other in the eating booth salvaged from Ramon's, the restaurant next to the Ganado post office, before it burned down ten years ago.

"When sheep go out, they go in a line," Edison said. "They know where the water is and you're just following. The newborns come. There is laughter. Play. And there's death. So sheep gave me that intensity of living.

"You know there's that physical aspect of things. All that crap. But even from a young age, I learned from the sheep, there's *something out there.* I'd see a mesa and wonder, 'What's over the line of that mesa?' And I think that to this day. So it's a bit more philosophical. It's more than the physical. Something's Out There. That was it for me. Gotta go get it."

This feeling was unique from his parents and siblings. They all repeat that he did not get it from them.

"I think it was subconsciously articulated from the sheep," he said.

We talked about the preparation. This kind of long-distance running breaks down to four things: Your inner soul. Your heart. Your cognitive thinking—the mapping of the terrain, the roll of the landscape. And the well-being of the psyche—you feed, eat well, get your glucose.

He hoped this preparation made him worthy of the run.

"The Diné people who survived that Long Walk maintained the elegance of who they were, even though they were tormented by their experience," Edison said. "My songs. I need to bring that back to Navajoland. Can I manage that? Am I the person for that? They did."

Edison told the story of how he'd once raced at Wichita State. It was the championship race with twenty-nine teams. It was so hot and so humid that no one could post a fast time. The top ten runners were all Native Americans that day.

"We're just so durable," Edison said. "We're used to this gut-wrenching. This process here. And that was so profound to me."

He said he knew this run would be his last ultrarun.

"This is it. I *know*," he said. "This is closure. As a person, it will be a review of things for me. It will be a teaching kit. And to leave something behind for the people. It is one person leaving behind their lifeline."

I ask him if he's nervous. He sips his coffee.

"I'm actually just going through the motions," he said. "The rest of it is done. It's all done."

He points to my notebook. "Even *that* is done."

The crickets sing in the grass. Heat rises in wavy air from the red mesas to the north. The highway screams.

Edison applies his lip balm while bouncing his legs in the camping chair.

"It's really beautiful up there. Very scenic," he says. He rubs lotion on his nose. "It's going to cook my nose today. I can feel it." He stands and looks at Jay-Lynn.

"This is what you can tell your friends that you did with your summer," he says. "You can say, 'I took the slowest trip to Santa Fe *ever*.'"

He laughs. Edison is running.

The Americans take Santa Fé without firing a shot. They bribe their way into power after paying nearly twenty-five thousand dollars in gold to Governor Manuel Armijo to "submit to Fate" and surrender the country, and he does. The celebrated American horseman and dragoon commander, Col. Stephen Watts Kearny, is no fool. He cannot keep the province by force of arms. He will be moving on to stamp down revolt and lay claim to California, where veins of ore will pull over one hundred thousand men from one side of the continent to the other in less than ten years. He decides the Americans will create an ally of the Mexicans by creating a common enemy. This common enemy will be played by the Navajo tribe.

He calls a meeting where he states, "The Navajos come down from the mountains and carry off your sheep and your women whenever they please. My government will correct all this. They will keep off the Indians, protect you in your persons and property."[30]

Kearny orders a fort built on a hill north and east of the city so that the city sits in sight of his cannons. Fort Marcy now commands a wide view of the bosque and the meanders of willow and grass running off toward the west to the Río Grande, swerving before the sloping dark shroud of the Jémez Mountains towering two miles into the sky.

While the Americans build the fort, Navajo warriors raid settlements along the Río Grande. Then they raid the Americans. Kearny is a cavalry man. He takes affront to the theft of his horses. Kearny summons Sandoval to him. Sandoval learns within minutes of how ignorant Kearny is of the politics of the region. A few days later, Sandoval reports that Narbona sends a summons from Navajo land and wishes to make peace. Kearny believes him.

But Narbona is not there. He is already at Santa Fé, in the mountains, behind the Americans, watching them from the cliffs. He sees them in regimental drills. They make parades. He watches their target practices with their 1817 model percussion cap rifles, hears the thunder of smoke from their cannon volleys. They have defeated the Mexicans in mere weeks. Their clothing shines with brass. They are gun men.

He cannot have these men as enemies.

He returns home to Tunicha Valley. The sort of men who follow *Hastiin Ch'il Haazhinii* (Man of the Black Reeds), who the Mexicans call Little Manuel, *Manuelito,* do not agree. To them, these Americans are another type of Mexican, only with better guns. This is not their first rodeo. They know when they meet and exchange words that most of those words are lies, and that any promises drift to the wind.

Edison doesn't sit in the chair. He keeps moving another two miles. Manufactured homes tilt on their weak foundations between reedy Siberian elms next to dilapidated, unlivable houses built along the previously bustling Route 66. But the world moved on, just a hundred yards over and fifty miles per hour faster to the Interstate Route 40. The trucks rumble and scream west. The crickets scream in the grass, until it is all one scream. Until the scream becomes a song Edison hears while he is running.

He stops. *Tsoodził* staggers to the sky.

Edison whispers, "Beautiful. There it is. It's thinking, 'Hey. What's all the fuss about?'" He takes water. He can't take Sobé anymore, so if I want any I can help myself. He also can't drink Gatorade. He's taking a premixed Arizona sweet tea now.

"I can really feel it here this morning," he says, rubbing the flexors, the psoas, the sartorius, and the other bundles of muscle around his crotch and inner legs. "You just want to moan from the pain. I know it's the age. You need to nurture it and really take care of it. If you don't maintain it, you have nothing left to take the weight. It all comes back to the water, the vitamins, the muscle. You've got to look after it. You've got to be smart."

Edison leans forward over his worn shoes. He looks to the mountain. "*This* is not smart."

Jason, Lorraine, and Jay-Lynn laugh.

"It's not," Edison says. "I mean, who comes up with this kooky idea?" He runs another two miles. He walks off the pain.

Edison had his checkup at Sage Memorial Hospital in Ganado medical center before this run. The nurse there took his vitals and his blood pressure.

"She couldn't believe it," Edison says. "She said, 'Your numbers are completely perfect. Perfect.' And she actually took them again. She couldn't believe it. She said, 'How old did you say you were again?' I said I was fifty-nine years old. She shook her head. She just couldn't believe it. She said, 'Well, whatever you're doing, keep doing it.' But she never asked me what I actually *did*. Which was a bit disappointing."

I ask what he would have told her if she had asked.

"Stay active," Edison says. "And move what you eat. You've got to use it. Just stay moving."

In the northern distance rises Haystack Mesa.

"I've been invited out there many times," Edison says. "I know an excellent silversmith from there named Ernest Rangel. He's half New Mexican and half Navajo. But he was raised by his mother. So he grew up speaking Navajo. He's actually a professional cowboy. He travels over to Europe to rodeo and then he'll come back here to Haystack. When you meet him, you'd never think he was Navajo. He's so light-complected. But one day I just had to ask him. '*Ha'íísh Diné?*' He said, ''*Aoo*.''"

Edison smiles. He is missing two teeth on the right side, back from his bicuspids.

He changes shoes during the rest. "I just felt like I was really pounding up there. Like I was just hurting."

He checks inside of the Avias. Nothing. He slips his feet into the blue and white Nikes. He doesn't change socks because his feet will have to be retaped. His feet will be wet and sweaty, but it's better to let it be.

Jason brings back the Avia shoe. One of the rubber pieces on the bottom has already stripped away.

He drinks his Arizona sweet tea. "There's something about it. That sweet and cold. I could just drink down two of these, no problem. But I have to watch it. I can't take too much."

He stops after ten miles. Edison starts eating salty sunflower seeds. They drive on to their hotel room in Grants, New Mexico.

An American captain, John Reid, follows Sandoval into the mountains with thirty Missouri volunteers at his command. The New Mexicans can't believe the audacity of the American. They say to "enter the Navajo country with less than an army was considered by them as certain destruction."[31]

Reid sees shadows of Navajo warriors watching from behind the piñon trees and the rimrock of the Chuska Mountains.

Thirty Navajo warriors ride down on them. They dismount their horses in fluid movements that impress the Missourians. The warriors have tied eagle feathers in their hair and in their war bonnets. Many wear helmets sewn together from the scalps of mountain lions. They ride muscular, groomed horses. They are men of prowess.

Ten Diné women ride with them, dressed in fine blankets and splendid clothing. Many Missourians admire the women's delicate feet, their long black hair, their brass bracelets. The women saddle their own horses with no help from their men.

Reid leads his men deeper into Navajo country and realizes by the end of the first day that his men are outnumbered a hundred to one. By the next day, they are surrounded by thousands of Navajo warriors and women. They watch the October sun set into the ponderosa pines on the ridges of the Chuska Mountains. That is when Narbona arrives.

He is thin and bent in the saddle. The American captain finds him mild and amiable. Narbona has grown his nails very long, over an inch. The claws are sharp enough to rip out the captain's throat. The American captain has thirty men at his command. The Navajo riders encircle them. Narbona has at least a thousand. Before he pulls on his rein to stop his horse, he realizes he and his men are totally in Narbona's power.

One of Narbona's men offers to take the captain's horses to graze in a pasture. The pasture is five miles away. The captain believes the Navajo to be the "most savage and proverbially treacherous" people on the continent. They are a race of horse thieves.

The captain gives over the reins.

That night, the Missourians wander into something like a carnival or Navajo rendezvous, a festival where Navajo men compete and gamble in long-jumping, stone throwing, archery, stick-dice, and horse racing. The Americans show off their revolvers to the warriors. One soldier wears a watch and when the Navajo warriors place it to their ears, the ticking sound makes them hop backward as though they'd put their head against the mouth of a rattlesnake.

Then the music plays from shells and timbrels and the people begin to dance. Five hundred Navajo people dance in the hollow of the mountains. Americans strapping revolvers, muskets, and boot knives join the dance.

The men get to know each other. They enjoy the suck of fat from the lamb shanks grilled over fires. They spontaneously dance with each other. They trade clothing. A finely beaded buckskin shirt for a wool coat.

One volunteer on the expedition wrote that it was "truly romantic."

Many Navajo children would have benefited from that night lasting one hundred and fifty years.

The American captain steps into a council with Narbona and his most trusted family and advisors. Narbona has killed and scalped many Mexicans. But he knows his time is coming. He is well into his winter. He wants a peace. He calls the American captain and his soldiers *Diné Doleel, Personas Nuevas*. The New Men.

Manuelito sees the Americans as only new types of Mexicans. The only woman in the council is Narbona's wife. She says there are only a few of these New Men. They should just attack and kill them.

In the morning, every American horse comes back from the pasture. The captain says the visit was mostly "pleasurable excitement." He finds the Diné to be clever breeders of horses. He compares them to the Tartars. They bring "devastating incursions" against the Mexicans. The Navajo are the "Lords of the Mountains."[32]

Debates will thunder from the East from buildings of geometrically precise stone ornamented with wood planed and shaped to the golden ratio, as though it might resurrect an idealized democracy of Greece or a republic of Rome. They will argue whether people can be property or not. In less than ten years, the nine men of the Supreme Court will decide that they can be.

If any Americans wonder whether this part of Mexico would lean to a free or slave state, an American lieutenant—a topographical engineer who calculates landscapes by how well they might be used to send death by artillery—settles the question. He winds up in New Mexico. He rides through sand and sparse grass with the American captain to meet Narbona to arrange the treaty. They stop at a ranch between

Bernalillo and Santo Domingo. He bargains for a mule. He is also offered to buy a Navajo woman working on the ranch.[33]

That afternoon, National Public Radio talks about a new book, *The Brain Defense* by Kevin Davis. The book examines the case of Herbert Weinstein, a sixty-five-year-old, quiet, self-contained mensch who had retired from a career as an advertising executive. He had no criminal record. No history of violent behavior. But that didn't stop him from grabbing his wife by the throat during an argument. He squeezed until she died. Then he dragged her body to a window of their twelfth-story apartment at East 72nd St. He dropped her body out the window to make it look like suicide. It was 1991.

Weinstein's attorney thought this was so odd that he ordered an MRI on Weinstein's skull. The scan revealed a cyst the size of an orange on Weinstein's frontal lobe, the part of the brain that physicians believe governs judgment and impulse control. Weinstein's attorney argued that the man could not be held criminally responsible for the murder. It was the first case in the United States where "a judge allowed a scan showing a defendant's brain activity to be admitted as evidence to support a claim of innocence."

Then comes a story of how the World Health Organization has deemed video game addiction as "gaming disorder."

Then comes the story of Army Specialist Robert Joseph Allen. He died by suicide at a time when more soldiers were slaying themselves than dying by bullets from the enemy. He spent most of his time driving Stryker armored vehicles in the streets of Iraq. When he came home, his mom noticed he had symptoms of PTSD, like paranoia and sleeplessness. When he did sleep, he had nightmares about burning alive inside his Stryker vehicle.

Allen killed himself in 2012 while based at Fort Lewis near Seattle. He had two sons. He was twenty-seven years old.

His mother had to explain to her son's child, "Daddy died from war because he had a very sad heart."

She remembers when he got off the plane after returning from Iraq. "I thanked God he made it home safe. I didn't realize that he didn't. I feel like he's not looked at as a hero because his wounds weren't immediate and they weren't physical. And aside from losing my son, that's probably one of the most painful things."

In the traditional beliefs, there is a part of you that can never find harmony in the world. This spirit is a black distillation of menace—what Jungian psychologists might call a *shadow-self*—that men like Narbona called a *ch'įįndii*. This is the part of you that gets left behind after you die. It has never lived and so it cannot go into the spirit world and live forever. It is the spirit always bending you toward death. It is an idea.

What can we say of them? These dark things inside our minds?

We meet again at the road. Edison is ready to move again in his green Nike shirt. He seems to have a clearer energy about him. He has taken a full meal for the first time in days. Italian bread, chicken, mashed potatoes, gravy, all from the Denny's in Grants.

Edison likes Route 66. Not too busy. Low speed. Everyone else likes it, too. He walks to the road. A Hispanic man guns past on a motorcycle with a woman riding passenger behind. He makes no hesitation or attempt to give room. A bone-white human skull stands out in bas-relief from the black leather passenger seat rest. It watches from the tailpipe of the racing motorcycle as Edison takes his stride.

The skull says nothing.

Joe Lunny, the photographer documenting Edison and the run, has said that one thing Edison wants to do if he reaches the state capital, the Roundhouse in New Mexico, is to ask, "*Why? Why* did this Long Walk have to happen?" Who knows what the state reps will say. The skull on the back of the motorcycle seems to know the answer.

The first two miles come like a dance. Edison takes water. He runs as a train passes. It is over 150 cars long. The cars are double-stacked with shipping containers filled with packaged foods, deck screws, canned tomatoes, baby diapers, and rifle ammunition. All artifacts and testaments to the American civilization, for which the Diné had to be cleared from their land.

Each car stretches fifty standard feet. It would take Edison about ten minutes to run its mile-and-a-half length.

The wind bends the blond grass. We come in full distance from Prewitt, New Mexico. We pass the Tomahawk Lounge.

Edison jokes about his memories of the Tomahawk. "It'll be midnight and can't kick them out of there," he hee-haws. "Whew-ee."

He descends a slight downhill. Edison breaks his stride. He shakes the rattle to the sky. He dances forward with the rattle to the wildflowers—the white daisy, the scarlet globemallow—growing beside the road. He shakes the rattle to the sky. He shakes it to the four directions. He is running into souls. He shakes the sobs and tears of the people who passed the blue mountain on the way to some unfamiliar destiny where their gods might abandon them.

The rattle shakes. Edison dances in the road. He holds the rattle to the mountain. He waves it back and forth. The souls are here.

He turns and looks at me. He runs to the window of the Prius. He shakes the rattle. He hands it to me.

"That one was for you, buddy," he says. He runs east. I shake the rattle. This is a comfort. For the patient. Maybe that's the souls. Maybe that's Edison. Maybe that's me.

American officers swallow the Mexican magic realism of the Navajos and vomit these fabrications in the places of debate in the wet, green world of the East. The story goes like this: Navajos descend to carry off fruit and sheep, women and children from the Mexicans on the Río Grande, and the Mexicans weep and gnash their teeth and shake their fists at the mountains and they never pursue the Navajo, never, out of fear and they have never armed expeditions and they have never hunted Navajo children to sell as slaves and the Mexicans are clean and pure and New Mexicans now and the Navajos are dirty and the Navajos steal because they do not know how to grow their own corn or squash or peaches and do you see, señor? It was all the governor's fault, Manuel Armijo, and he has a power over the Navajo and he is a sorcerer of the Navajo and he never allowed the Mexicans to war on the Navajo and we hated Armijo, no? and if we offended him, he would send the Navajos against us. Don't you see, señor? Don't you see?

Kearny sees. He is one of the New Men. The past is wiped away. In October 1846, he publishes permission for Mexicans to retaliate and make war on Navajos. They can "march into the country of their enemies, the Navajos, to recover their property, to make reprisals, and obtain redress for the many insults received from them."[34]

Kearny knows the way of it. If he and the New Mexicans have a common enemy, they have a common interest. The more time New Mexicans spend trying to murder and enslave Navajos, the less time they have to kill the Americans who have just occupied them and whom they vastly outnumber.

I shake the rattle. Edison runs back to the window, and I hand it off to him. A train blares and pushes thirty thousand tons of freight to the West. *Tsoodził* stands 11,306 feet into the sky and calls for rain. The heat blankets the blond grass.

The run continues until we hit two miles. Edison sits in his chair. He takes water and faces south in the shade of the Armada.

"Thank you for that," I say.

"'*Aoo*'," he nods. "It's for the duration. The blue mountain. The thinking process."

"*Nahaata*'," I say.

"'*Aoo*'." He stands out of the chair. Lorraine makes a joke about running along the road with Edison, like we are all running in a still life alongside him. He walks to the edge of the asphalt.

"In Navajo, they say, '*Be atiin baa'lizhiin Dii éí ligai. Díílitso'íí.*' You are running the black road." He points to the lines painted on the road. "There is the white, the color of the white shell of the East. There is the yellow, the color of *tádídíín,* the sacred corn pollen. These are the colors of the four directions."

Black. White. Yellow. Look up and you see a depth of blue you cannot escape.

These colors Edison painted on his body when he started from Spider Rock. East. South. West. North. They have all been there, over the more than six hundred thousand miles I've driven as an adult, and I never noticed them. Now I see them. See them forever.

A train passes. Edison sticks out his thumb, as though hitchhiking. "Do you think he'll stop?" he jokes.

He runs another two miles. Past Siberian elms growing through the rusted hoods of abandoned trucks along Route 66. The Siberian elm is a growing hymn of the tenacity of life. I have seen it grow from the bottoms of storm drains, through sewer grates, to find the light. Its seeds scatter in the wind and find any crack from which they can grow. People cut them back. They keep growing. The Siberian elm demands its own life. We call it an invasive species.

The dogs run to the fences of the manufactured homes, the adobe casitas, the land plots for sale. The dogs just love Edison. He is a beautiful kind of prey.

At the next stop, Edison says he should pose for a photo.

"The many tribes. The Apache. The Hopi. The Pueblos. The Navajos. They will appreciate that very much."

Joe takes the shots. Edison says the bottom of the photo should read just one thing: "Mt. Taylor." To the east, Cebolleta mesa rises to the blue sky.

A month later, American troops at Abiquiú meet up with Americans from Cebolleta at *Shash Bitó,* where a sixteen-year-old Manuel Chaves had pulled the arrows from his body. An American colonel, Alexander Doniphan, rides in with his Missouri volunteers.

Doniphan understands the strange lands of justice. He is best known in Missouri for his defense of the Mormons and their families during a small civil war that broke out in 1838. Doniphan led the state militia against the Mormons, though he believed the Mormons were only defending their families. Once their prophet, Joseph Smith, surrendered, Doniphan brought him in. The general of the militia then convicted Smith of treason and ordered Doniphan to execute Smith and his followers.

Doniphan refused to follow the order. "It is cold-blooded murder," he said. "I will not obey your order. If you execute these men, I will hold you responsible before an earthly tribunal, so help me God."

Joseph Smith and his Mormon followers fled the state to settle in Illinois. Smith named one of his sons Alexander in honor of Doniphan.

Doniphan sends a runner. The runner tells the tribal chieftains to meet. Doniphan lays it out. The Americans now own the ground. The Navajos have become their "red children."

A young *naat'áanii* named *Nataałith* stands from the sand. A Mexican interpreter says his name is Zarcillos Largos (Long Earrings). He says the Americans have "a strange cause of war against the Navajos." They have a common enemy in the Mexicans. The Americans have merely done what the Navajos have tried for over a century. They have humbled and conquered the Mexicans.

This impresses many Navajos. They see themselves in the Americans.

Zarcillos Largos asks that they let the war play out: "Look how matters stand. This is *our war*. We have more right to complain of you for interfering in our war than you have to quarrel with us for continuing a war we had begun long before you got here. If you will act justly, you will allow us to settle our own differences."[35]

Doniphan must explain. There is no more Mexico here. There are no more Mexicans. The war is over. All of that has been swept away. There are only Americans now.

A dove lands in an oak thicket. It rustles the leaves and chirps. Horses snort in the grass. Zarcillos Largos raises an eyebrow. He thinks Doniphan is wrong. Zarcillos Largos is right.

Doniphan offers Navajos the old American deal, where they can go into their sacred lands, hunt down animals, skin them. Go out into the wilds of the mountains. Find their sacred animals. Trap them. Beat them to death. Skin them. Bring us the furs for goods that must be smelted from ores and cooked by forges that devour the sacred.

Doniphan offers to teach them how to make leather saddles, bullets, and wagons. He asks if any of the Diné want to join him to fight and kill Mexicans in Chihuahua.

Doniphan is impressed with the Diné. They are a warrior people. They have immense herds. They are intelligent and keep good order. The men and women look eye to eye with each other.

"They are handsome, well made, and in every respect a highly civilized people, being as a nation of a higher order of beings than the mass of their neighbors, the Mexicans," he says. "They are certainly the noblest of the American aborigines."[36]

Narbona and the Diné sign the treaty with Doniphan. None volunteer to fight the people in Chihuahua. The Navajos do not know them and so have no reason to fight them. There is one sticking point of the treaty. The Navajos want their children back from the Mexicans. The Americans promise to return them. They do not.

Doniphan and his Missouri volunteers march south to kill Mexicans. Just south of Socorro, one of their Mexican shepherds goes missing and eight hundred sheep with him. Two soldiers go out to find the sheep.

Other Missourians find them six miles to the west. The two men's bodies puff in the heat. Flies land on the Navajo arrows punched through their bodies. Their faces have been broken and smashed with stones.

This is *Los Dueños del Mundo*'s answer to Doniphan's treaty.

Motorcycles shoot past.

"*Tł'idi. Tł'idi*," I say, and I make a farting noise with my lips. Everyone laughs. *Tł'idi* is the Navajo word for "motorcycle." It literally means, "The Farter," because of the sound it makes. A Navajo man must stray far from his language indeed to think that straddling a hog somehow swells his testicles or straightens his spine. What would the skull on the back of the leather seat say to that?

Edison runs another two miles. The Nikes take the drumming well. We get toward the stop. Edison claps his hands together. He walks up in a bright mood, smiling against the pain.

"So. I was living on the East Coast, right? Traveling through New England. Working. Trying to figure it out. When I was looking for a place, people would say, 'Well, you take Route 10 five miles and take off-ramp 35. Take a right at the Dairy Queen across from the car dealership. You'll see a credit union across from a diner and you know you've gone too far. So, years later, I come back here to the Rez. I was driving to Torreón, New Mexico. They invited me to speak at their graduation. I drove out there. And something happened. I don't remember what. Something with traffic. I was stuck waiting and I was late."

The wind drifts Edison's gray hair under his hat, across his yellow glasses.

"I checked the clock, and I was behind by eight minutes. I thought, 'I have got to find this place. I have eight minutes.' So I was driving and I saw this old woman running sheep along the road. I pulled over and asked her how to get to the school. And we're speaking in Navajo. This is an old Navajo woman. Very deliberate. She says, 'You see this fence? Follow this fence. You'll come to a cattle guard. Go one more. Turn right and drive over the cattleguard. You will see powerlines. Follow them. At the eighth pole, turn right, and it will get you there.' And it did! I got there. Gave the speech. 'Follow Route 10 and take exit 35?' What was I thinking over there? I was lost."

Edison had worked at Yale University as a restoration and construction worker, earning a decent salary. On weekends, he would compete in road races on the East Coast between Boston and New York City. Some weekends he would buy a train ticket and ride the Amtrak from New Haven to New York and then to Washington, DC, just to see the buildings and watch people. The Americans on parade in the ever-changing America. A humbling site.

He walks to front of the Armada. He jokes about how his "shoosh" are hurting him. It is hot. The sweat builds. It was a cloudless sky today, the air over ninety degrees. I say to Edison that I will go to the mountain and ask for some clouds for tomorrow.

"'Aoo'. A double helping, please." He sips water. "It's time to eat. And to sleep. You know something, I have never worked so hard in my life to *rest*."

He laughs and so do we all.

"I mean it," he says. "On the other runs, I would fall asleep no problem. Like a baby. Now, it's hard. *Hagooshii' la'*."

Joe Lunny, the videographer, and I linger to do an interview about the run. The blood-light falls over *Tsoodził*. It dyes the mountain in the shades I have seen on *Dził daní'áhígíí To'woł* in Taos. We use our time and the last light captures what I have to say.

He asks me why Edison is doing the run.

I say that the run is a kind of prayer that you can't make with words. So you make the prayer with your body because the prayer goes beyond what words can say.

A green Geo Metro hatchback pulls up. An attractive Navajo woman in a turquoise blouse with dark hair that falls to her back steps out of the passenger side.

"Excuse me," she coos politely. "We were wondering what this run is all about."

Joe and I explain as a strongly built Anglo man with gray hair pulled into a ponytail steps out of the Metro. I am surprised he can fit into it. He walks in jeans and a green button-up work shirt. He exchanges handshakes with one of his mitts. He introduces himself as John Boomer. The woman is Beverly Billiman. Her father, Howard Billiman Jr., was a Navajo codetalker with the second group who fought in the Pacific against the Japanese.

They have come from the Dairy Queen at Bluewater Village, New Mexico, to celebrate John's fiftieth year of living in Navajo Country—"Dinétah," as he calls it. He taught at the Rough Rock Demonstration School between 1968 and 1972. Then he got into woodworking and other arts. He worked at the Crystal Trading Post. Beverly is from Sawmill, Arizona. When I explain how I grew up in Ganado, we laugh. We are practically neighbors.

John lives just outside Milan, New Mexico. He points to the mountain. "If you can see those two water towers there, I'm almost in the middle."

"That means he glows in the dark," Beverly jokes.

"Yeah, I'm irradiated," John says. "I live inside the super-fund site, where those uranium mines had been sunk at the base of the mountain. If you look there." He points to the horizon, now purple and gold and scarlet with the afterglow of sunset. The Diné call this *náátsʼíílid* (the rainbow).

"That little mesa there, the blond-colored one? That's about 220 million tons of uranium mine tailings," he says. "The Anaconda mine was just out there. And we had the Jackpile Mine over there. It was the largest open-pit uranium mine in the world at that time.* They were out here crushing rock all the time."

He explains he's just been on a tour with a state geologist who'd laid out the locations of the mines, how they've begun to detect radiation in the groundwater under Milan, how the uranium was first discovered out by the mesa on the west horizon called Haystack, where Edison's silversmithing, cowboying friend first learned to rope and ride before shipping off to Europe, where a local named Paddy Martínez discovered the first evidence of the pitchblende ore in 1951. From there, the digging and smashing was on. The crushed pitchblende shipped to a place in northern New Mexico, somewhere on the Pajarito Plateau. Why? Who the fuck cares? I just bought this here new truck. And so it went until people saw the photographs of some fire deity straddling the skies above Japan, flaying alive more than 160,000 of those nip-bastards in a single day and didn't they have it coming.

The skull grins from the back of the motorcycle. It doesn't say a word. It doesn't have to.

Boomer has pushed and pushed with his volunteer group MASE (Multicultural Alliance for a Safe Environment). They've had testing done on water movement around the wells in Milan, tested the background radiation left by the trucks that hauled the rock to Gallup or to the train spur. A guy was out in Boomer's backyard just a few weeks ago from *National Geographic,* taking photos of the mountain with a special camera that can photograph any radiological signature higher than background radiation. Something in me never wants to see those images.

He's pushed with his neighbors to have the water tested. They're all unpaid volunteers. They are showing up after work. Boomer got tired. So he stepped away from it.

While he speaks, Beverly tells Joe a story of how she also grew up

---

* The Jackpile Mine, discovered in the early 1950s, once employed over eight hundred people, mostly Natives from Laguna Pueblo. It pulled 24 million tons of pitchblende (uranium ore) from the ground and left behind 400 million tons of radioactive tailings and rock.

running. She once went running in the morning and had a jackrabbit jump out in front of her and kick her in the head in the predawn light.

Before I leave the road, I look to *Tsoodził*. I thank the mountain for this day. I ask for clouds for Edison.

In the morning, the clouds are there.

The Americans occupy Santa Fé. The mounted Missouri kids are loud. They are conquerors. The New Mexicans taste the conquest they once brought to the region. The taste is bitter. The Americans have not had the decency to ride out and annihilate the Navajos.

The revolt comes in Taos in January 1847 after Taos Pueblo natives protest the arrest and jailing of some of their friends on charges they believe unfair. The civil governor dismisses them. They attack his house under the winter stars until they have shot him full of arrows. The governor is alive when a Taos Pueblo man walks in and scalps him with the string of his bow. They beat him and knife him in front of his family and leave him with an arrow sticking out of his face. Then they take his gray-haired scalp and nail it to a plank like the hide of an animal.

The American district attorney is caught, tied up, stabbed blind with knives, then thrown into a ditch with hungry pigs. They eat him while he stumbles and screams his last breaths as steam into the cold air. The Taos natives and Mexicans laugh and cheer.

But really this is all a question.

The Americans bring an answer.

They ride up over the meadows in the mountain pass east of Taos. One of the men in the army is a black man named Dick Green. He was the civil governor's slave. He rides north to avenge his master's death.

The four hundred men stamp through thick snow. They murder unarmed farmers by the dozens if they don't run away. They drive the natives and the locals into the church at the Taos Pueblo. The Mexicans and natives of Taos Pueblo hold up inside the church's thick adobe walls. The Americans ax through them, stick the barrels of their howitzer into the breaches, and fire until all they hear is the crying of children beneath the dead bodies of their parents. The Taos Mountain rises a mile up from the piñon-pine forest. Clouds swirl around its snow-swept peaks. It says nothing; it doesn't have to. The crows and ravens eat the dead. The bodies of two hundred Taos Pueblo natives go under ground.

One of the Americans—a mountain man who volunteers for the expedition—sees a Mexican man walk out of a sagebrush thicket to surrender. He yells that he likes Americans. The mountain man throws a small sword at the man's feet and says that he must run off and stab some Mexicans if he loves Americans so much. The Mexican walks into the trees and stabs one of his dead compatriots with the sword. He brings back the blade dripping with blood.

The mountain man tells him that if he would kill one of his own people he must know nothing of loyalty. He shoots the man and leaves him to die on the cold ground.

The survivors in Taos call the Americans Los Diablos Americanos. The wolves howl at night.

That is the answer.

Mural depicting Diné chieftain Manuelito on a cinder-block utility shed at the local gas company. Artist unknown. Chinle, Arizona. Photo by Jim Kristofic.

The Diné watch this reckless American carnage unfold from the distance of their raiding trails into Taos. They are unimpressed.

That spring, the Navajo young men kill seven. One is Juan Cruz Pino, a son of a well-known rancher who keeps many Navajo slaves. Local Mexicans walk into dusty offices at Fort Marcy above Santa Fé. The boards creak beneath their feet as they shout their dreams of a land where the wolves are murdered away, the mountain lions are hunted to the last hide, and the Navajos are hunted to extinction or pass totally into slavery. And the Kingdom of the Lord will come without end. Amen.

By March 1848, the new American commander allows slave raids to begin again into Navajo country. The Americans can do nothing against the Navajo. Most of their troops are infantry. The Navajos gallop away on their horses and their dreams. The commander strikes paper with Narbona and other *naat'áanii*. Nothing is honored. Narbona and his men know it is a sham. The Diné are adopting a name for the Americans. Bellicanas. *Biligaanas.* The Fighters.

There is another meaning in the name. Some say *Bilání joghal'ndi*— They Are Many and Keep Coming.

When we meet, I tell Edison about how John and Beverly stopped to talk with Joe and me, about the Church Rock uranium slowly working its way into the groundwater from the worst nuclear accident in United States history. The Church Rock incident happened just before dawn on the night of July 16, 1979, when the United Nuclear Corporation's mine-tailings pond opened a twenty-foot breach in the earth berm. This breach formed because the tailings pond—like every tailings pond on the Navajo Nation—was already leeching millions of gallons of water contaminated by acids, metals, and uranium tailings into the ground and the Río Puerco. These are just estimates. No one knows the real number. No one wants to know.

See it. The cool air in the July morning fills with blue light on the black horizon. A dove chirps as it lands on the piñon. A darkling beetle creeps down an ant hill. Then the roar of water and the poisoning has begun. 94 million gallons of radioactive sludge goes down into the Río Puerco. The flood can fill 140 Olympic-sized swimming pools. The

Edison running. Drawing by Edison's oldest daughter, Emry Eskeets, age eleven, April 21, 2001

onrush twists a metal culvert. Radiation slays sheep almost immediately as they drink from the stream. Crops wither along the river. The radioactive flood roils more than fifty miles downstream.

All the poisons sink below the ground. Some are still there and others are traveling in the aquifers. They will never leave.[37]

Some travel in the organs of Diné people. Their lungs and kidneys speak this story in tumors. The tumors say nothing. They don't have to. Perhaps the skull on the motorcycle knows the language.

This was only the Church Rock incident, the spill the company couldn't keep hidden. Edison remembers several spills and radioactive flows that the company simply hid by covering in dirt. Or they would simply tell people to avoid the water.

"I remember all of that," Edison says. "There was quite a bit of mining here. They would break up the rocks right here. Truck them over to Grants. All that dust was just trailing behind on the wind and on the road. You've heard of that Church Rock mine spill? Of course, we played in that. We played in that damned water. And no one even told us."

He shakes his head and glances down the road at the abandoned houses, roofs bowed by snow and heat and rain.

"So they are dealing with what's left of that mining," he says. "Now here with these abandoned houses. This is the closure."

He walks into the run. He's wetted his red bandana to keep his mouth moist. I ask if he's drinking room-temperature water. He is. Sometimes he'll take cold water to shock his system.

He runs through Grants. He passes the Memorial Day Park. People wave from the flea market. "Good morning!" a Navajo woman calls. People stop working at the tire shop to watch Edison run past. The main street is a motley of vacancies, but the town has kept the Adult Video store at bay. The hotels stand abandoned. The mining museum is open. The 1st Street Café set up in the old McDonald's building is closed. A guy with long sideburns races by in a black Dodge Charger.

"That guy knows how to drive," Edison says. "We get it. Thank you."

Tsoodził shines blue and green in the cool morning. Edison sits after we cross over the train tracks.

"It didn't seem like much was happening in the center of town, which is disappointing," he says.

Lorraine wears a Captain America shirt with the red, white, and blue shield styled in patterns of roses, Indigenous swirls, and snowflake patterns.

"I'm wearing it for Memorial Day," she says. "We used to read all those comic books. We'd get them at the 7-2-11 store in Gallup. Back then, we didn't have running water or electricity. We didn't have AC or anything like that. So in the evening we would share those comic books. 'Hey! Let me read that one!' And we'd just squabble over them!"

It should surprise no one that Diné people might feel some kinship with the cursed heroes of the Marvel Universe, each betrayed by science but somehow enhanced by it. Born of lab experiments gone wrong. Each made a wanderer and a god by their individual Church Rocks.

And now there is Edison. *Jau'di'*. The Runner.*

Edison burps at the next rest. He reminds Lorraine that they need to change out the water. It tastes salty and it's giving his muscles problems. She asks if his stomach is okay. Edison says he's fine.

"I had the banana this morning," he says. "Sometimes the banana will make that bloating. Sometimes it doesn't. This time it did."

He sits and rubs his ankle. "I've been kicking at that ankle again," he says. He's taped moleskin over the spot where it's hurting. He's hoping the space and tension will help the chaffing recover before it becomes a blister.

"It's funny. In my home we always had a story," he says. "You know how old people wear sweatpants? And they'll wear them high up past their waist. My daughter said to me, 'Dad, the day I see you doing that I'm going to have to take you out back and put you down.' And one time I did that. I came in wearing a huge sweatpant pulled up to my armpits. She just got red in the face." He laughs at the memory. "Okay. Time to eat."

---

* A poetic word for a runner in Diné is *jádí*, the One Who Uses Legs or The Runner. This usually refers to the pronghorn antelope. The word *jau'di'* (pronounced something like: "JOW-DEH") refers specifically to a ceremonial runner. It is an old word, mostly left behind in the sands of long ago.

He steps gingerly into the Armada and Jason and Lorraine drive to McDonalds.

A year passes. An American commander named Col. J. M. Washington musters nearly four hundred men, a slice of American mercenaries and Mexicans. Many of the Mexicans own Navajo slaves. Washington is a veteran of the wars against the Creeks and the Seminoles. He seems aloof to his officers. Others call him reserved. He is not known for his laugh.

He marches out from Santa Fé with over two hundred troops. Half of them are Mexicans and Pueblo Indians. They bring the model 1841 percussion-lock rifles that broke the Mexican army in the war, two types of cannons, thirty days rations, and tents. They travel to Jémez and then turn to reach Canyon de Chelly. Local Navajos run away as the Americans and Mexicans burn their *hoghans* and cut down their cornfields.

As the Americans ride west into the country, Navajo warriors surround them. Some are nearly naked and wear only breechcloths. One man's naked body has been smeared in thin white paint.

The Navajo ride to the mountains ahead of the Americans. The Americans ride up to the Tunicha mountains behind the Navajo. A dark cloud hovers over the mountain. Lightning spears the peaks and flashes in the folds of cloud with an eerie turquoise light.

Members of Narbona's band ride in with livestock to appease Washington. The women herd them, riding with their babies tied up behind them in the *awee'tsaał* (cradleboard). The Americans and Mexicans introduce themselves as friends. The Navajos see the smoke from their smoldering *hoghans* and see what's left of their cornfields. The truth of American friendship is obvious.

Narbona and his ally José Largo make a deal. They give the Americans over a thousand sheep and cattle and ask that they leave their cornfields. Washington agrees to meet with Narbona. The old chieftain rides down to the American camp with nearly a thousand warriors. The wind tosses the eagle feathers at the tops of their fur caps. Their caps are shaped like helmets. Some are made from the scalps of mountain lions and the eyes of the cats drop down directly over the eyes of the warriors.

Their arrow quivers are made from mountain lion hides, and the long tails of the cats hang from the ends of the quivers and trail behind.

These are men who know they are lions.

Several officers meet Narbona. His face and his poise remind them of portraits of General George Washington hanging in the White House. Narbona leads the column through the pines and grass to the base of the mountains at Tuntsa Wash. When they arrive, the Americans destroy every cornfield they see.

They schedule a meeting for the next day.

Washington speaks through an interpreter. The Indian agent with him has no experience. He is a Georgia man and an appointee to the position. He tells Narbona, "If any wrong is done them by a citizen of the United States or by a Mexican, he or they shall be punished by the United States, as if the wrong had been done by a citizen of the United States, and on a citizen of the United States."

He notices that one of the Diné warriors has red hair and that his skin is fair. This white man is likely a captive taken by the Navajo many years ago. Now he rides with them.

They agree to meet at Canyon de Chelly to strike paper together.

After the council, Sandoval, the Diné who is not a Diné, the Diné who is something else, who captures other Diné and sells them in the plazas of Santa Fé, this man explains the terms of the council. And then he lets loose. He cusses at the Diné warriors, who steal into Mexican lands, who have visited the black-powder wrath of European slavers on his people in the shadows of the Blue Mountain. While he speaks, Washington's troops do a peculiar thing of loading powder into the long barrels of the cannons. During this harangue, a Mexican man or it is a Pueblo Indian man or some person who will never be known tells Washington that one of the horses among the Navajo is his stolen horse. It is all the same story. Someone lies and asks for something that was never theirs. They use their power as their evidence.

The colonel demands the horse. There is no proof required. The man on the horse kicks the animal's sides and they gallop away. Washington demands through the interpreter that the horse be returned or the Navajos will be shot. The Diné men see only the energy building. They know they will be shot. So they sprint away with the horses as Washington proves them right. The powder dies in flame. The cannons roar three times.

Narbona is hit four or five times. It is hard to tell from the ragged body cut to pieces. The Mexicans or the Puebloans in the militias (we are not sure) stand over his body and scalp him of his long white hair. Imagine an enemy standing over George Washington and scalping him. Feel that?

When the carnage settles, a civilian secretary who has tagged along with the expedition becomes disappointed that he has forgotten to cut off Narbona's head to preserve for a phrenologist friend back East.

After the morning run, I go to the mountain, to *Tsoodził,* the sacred blue mountain of the South, where the bluebirds fly, where the Great Ones, the *diyin dine'é,* placed the nest with eggs of turquoise.

The road to the summit passes by one of four state prisons built in Grants. Bluebirds flit past the chain-link perimeter fence and perch on the concertina wire.

The forest road that will take you up the mountain is easy to find. It has been recently graded and laid with fresh gravel. I could drive up most of the mountain in the Prius.

In the winter, I brought my sister, Yanabah, to the mountain to do an offering. She had just graduated from New Mexico State University with a nursing degree. The day before, she'd been commissioned as Second Lieutenant in the United States Army. She would serve as a psychiatric nurse in the army for the next six years.

They say that the Hero Twins had slain the first of the *Yé'iitsoh* on this mountain, that the thick, black lava rock around the mountain is the rivers of his black blood after the twins had severed his head. This was the place where the Hero Twins had made their first kill. It was a place where warriors made offerings to *Jóhonaa'éí* (The Sun) and the *diyin dine'é* (Great Ones) for protection and the courage to kill the enemy. So we went there. We put the turquoise and the bluebird feathers in a secret space in a cliff where water flowed. We took the soil from the place with reverence.

I was worried for Yanabah not because she might be sent overseas to a war. I was worried because she would be serving with other American soldiers. And if you're a woman serving in the military, you have a one in four chance of being sexually assaulted. That's called "rape" in the real world. And if you wanted to press charges, the commander investigating the whole affair could very likely be the same guy who raped you.

So I spent an hour showing her some jiu-jitsu techniques in the snow between the pines near the summit.

Today, I walk the trail we'd taken between oak and pine. The sun sits high and the shade is fleeting in the noon heat. I find the cliff and the offering is still there. I walk to the cliff and feel like I am trespassing. I have no turquoise to bring as offering this time.

I step from the cliff and walk down, when a red-breasted robin flies so close past my face that its feathers tap my eyelashes. I wonder how a bird could have flown so close and in such thick trees. Then I see the nest where the bird had exploded toward me. The nest is built no higher than my chest from the ground. I look inside. Three eggs bright blue as turquoise sit inside.

No need for an offering. The turquoise is already here. Message received. I belong.

I go down to another part of the mountain to nap. I wake and walk to a large meadow hidden by a long wall of pine. Tall ponderosas haunt the edge of the field with obvious signs of elk and deer herds bedding in the grass. I know Diné people had once hunted this place.

I find a pile of dark obsidian flakes—where someone had knapped arrowheads while preparing for a hunt. I take some to pay the *Jau'di'*. The Runner. For Edison.

Narbona's son-in-law, Manuelito, and Zarcillos Largos go on the war-path. Twenty miles away, an American mail carrier named Charles Malone encounters a party of Navajos. The Navajos leave him dead with arrows. The letters from the mailbag flutter in the sagebrush and sand. The Navajo war leaders decide to steal enough livestock to permanently impoverish the New Mexicans while Washington marches on to his peace conference at Canyon de Chelly. The Americans arrive and say the Diné have set fire to their homes as signals that the Americans are arriving when really the Mexican and Pueblo militia burn them. They meet at Canyon de Chelly. Promises float like ash and are gone.

A Mexican man rides into the American camp the next morning. Washington's secretary describes him as "a very active, intelligent-looking fellow." His dress and posture is like the Diné. He speaks only Navajo. He explains he had been captured by Navajos near Tecolote when he was thirteen years old. He now has two Navajo wives and three children. He still belongs to the *naat'áanii* Huerrero, who originally bought him.

He tells the Americans he is worried because he has heard the recent treaty demands the return of all captives. He explains that he does not wish to go back. His family is from Santa Fé. The Americans ask if they can take a message to them from the young man. The Mexican man wishes neither to speak with them nor hear from them.

At the camp, the Diné spread a rumor that Apache are attacking Zuni. Washington trots the men south. They reach Zuni and find a dead body outside the pueblo. The Zuni governor says it is a Navajo who they took captive after he tried raiding their sheep. After supper, the civilian secretary rides out to the corpse with the assistant surgeon, who packs a saw. He gets his head, after all.

At the Armada, I pass the obsidian flints to Jason, Lorraine, Jay-Lynn, and Edison.

Lorraine takes the slim obsidian and puts it in her coin purse, where she keeps her pale flint arrowhead.

"May our friendship last forever," she says.

Edison takes a small, pink neoprene patch from the pocket of his running shorts. Inside is a piece of white flint knapped into the sickle shape of a mountain lion claw. It has been with him since he started at Spider Rock.

"That's easily over five hundred years old," he says.

He found the white flint in northern Arizona during a run. He was walking outside, and the light reflected from the white stone. It seemed to say, 'Come here.' They greeted.

I ask what he thinks it might have been used for.

"I thought a lot about that," he says. "I think it comes from making the basket. When you take that yucca strand and you need to go right down the middle."

He makes the motion of holding the strand and creating a downward slice with the flint claw. "That's what it's mostly for, I think."

He slides the flint claw back into his pocket for the evening run. He gets out and sits in his chair to hydrate before the run. He bounces his legs and takes off his red Avia shoes. He's going to tape the sore at his ankle again.

"I've been kicking it. That spot. Your muscles can only take so much. They go so far. You ask them to do things, and they can't respond correctly anymore to the requests from the mind. So I put a few kicks into it and it's creating a sore. Then from all that pressure, that pounding, it will just get stretched and split. So you have to be careful. You have to take care of it."

He stands up and shakes out his arms. He doesn't speak. There's Something Out There.

Before he gets out of the chair, Jason offers him his two different tubes of Chap Stick. Edison points to the thick tube.

"That's just for stops." He takes the cherry-flavored red Chap Stick.

"There's your lady's red there," Jason jokes.

"You've got to look good in the road," Edison says. "You never know who you meet out there."

"This guy's all ready to go with his cherry-red," Lorraine laughs. "Just pampered."

Edison runs to Acoma.

The American expedition reaches Albuquerque a month later and marches back to Santa Fé. The Navajos have followed them. They invade the Río Grande valley. The next day, they kill five Mexicans at Sandía Pueblo. A week later, they kill a New Mexican within three miles of Santa Fé. They leave sixteen arrows in his back and two in his chest. The arrows are left as some answer that the New Mexicans somehow understand. People fear to travel more than ten miles outside Santa

Fé. Washington has taken the power of the American taxpayer and scattered it over the ground. He calls the expedition a show of might to establish the "foundation of a lasting peace."[38]

They bury the dead man in Santa Fé. No one knows what becomes of the arrows.

We come to the first stop at a crack in the volcanic rock that forms a canyon running east. A ridge of sandstone rises above the green swath.

"They slept here," Edison says as he strides into the next two miles. "This is where they laid it down for the night. Some laughter. A lot of tears."

He keeps pushing the downhill. He goes two miles under the *k'os t'aahíí* (thin clouds). The thermometer reads eighty-four degrees. It feels twenty degrees cooler than that. The *táshchozhii* (swallows) cut the air. Their wings curve into the shape of Edison's white flint, knapped and shaped in a time when no people in these sacred mountains had heard of a Spaniard.

A *ch'iyíít'ogii* (kingbird) calls from a Russian olive tree. A horse watches Edison run past, grass to its ankles, its black tail trailing in the breeze against the dark lava rock. Edison stops.

Water. Water to the red bandana on his wrist.

"We need to get Jay-Lynn to dress up as *Ye'íítsoh*," he says. "She can chase me. They'll see me running from you. 'There goes Edison. He just ran away like a little girl!'" He smiles.

"I wonder about that," he says. "The monsters. Whatever they were. The dinosaurs. Who knows? It's like we see those fossils. They were there. They *were here*. We should find out why. Most people look at it and say, 'Eeyah.'"

He makes a closing-down motion with his hands, as though dropping some invisible curtain.

"Eeyah. Dooda. But that's such a simple way of just shutting down your thinking process. Too much eeyaah. If the dinosaurs were there, why can't we incorporate them somehow? Why can't we make ceremonies and bring them in? Instead people say 'eeyah.' I see it all the time at the trading post. People bring in baskets and the rugs and they say you shouldn't talk about the tradition behind it. They say, 'Eeyah, don't do that.' Well, does a traditional person open a box of Nike shoes made in Vietnam by little kids for almost no wages? Look at that shirt you're wearing with that tag that says, 'Made in the Philippines.' You have that on you and their spirits where they were forced to make that are on you. It's not good. These traditional people made everything they wore. Their clothing. Everything. Their sweat is in that basket. Their food particles. Their stories. Everything. And you're going to say 'eeyah' to that? Almost everything in the store is traditional. You want it all to go into the closet or something?

"That's not to say there are not certain things at certain times that should not be talked about. There are some things that *are* 'eeyah.' That is there. There *is* 'eeyah.' But you have to decide how you take it in. But people will say, 'I'm going to sell you this basket, but you can't talk about it. That's *my* tradition.' That's just closed off. Enough with the damn 'eeyah'! We might as well call you dead, be buried in the ground. Then you'll never have to worry no more about 'eeyah.'

"What I'm saying is, it's the thinking process," he says. "The way you decide to proceed with an endeavor. The way you plan something into action. Like, this thing here."

He points at the Armada. "This machine is a *killer*. It's a death machine. It's a deadly weapon. The fuel in it. The speed. But if you approach it to say, 'You are a tool. I will use you for good, in a respectful way, to bring about a beneficial outcome.' Or some Navajo people will say, '*Baaschlichiin*,' about the highway. The road is almost like a telephone line. *Baas'jíínii* or *Baasjíín*. Eeyah. 'Oh the colors of the white, oh those sacred colors,' when they travel the highway. But these are roads of death! People die on these *all* the time!"

We had just passed a white metal cross reading: Bob Parsons, 1925–2009. A green sign with white lettering read: "Killed by a Drunk Driver."

We are looking out over the Cibola and McKinley country roads. They kill roughly fifty people every year.

"I mean, that's what really happens. Even this run. This run can be 'eeyah.' It's a *killer*. It wrecks your body. It just destroys your tissue. You couldn't do it forever. And so think about *that*. How do you incorporate that? To say, 'I'm going to use you in such a way as to make a balance, as to make a good way.' That is the way, for me. Some people just say 'eeyah,' and they are closed off from even thinking about it. I can't do that. That's when you go back to the taboo. The taboo is important. But there's the fear. That fear, man. I hate it."

Edison steps up to run and dances two miles. He drops down and across, following parallel with the highway. The black blood of the volcano.

At the next stop, he contemplates my front license plate. I received the plate from friends of mine who live near Ganado Lake. They say I am adopted into their clan. The *Tsénjíkíní* (Honey Comb Rock People). Some stories say this was the first clan and its people emerged from the walls of Canyon de Chelly in the place people now call White House Ruins, not far from Spider Rock.

"That goes back to *Nahasdzáán*," Edison says. "The earth is our mother."

The creation of peace means death by force in this country. The Americans build an outpost at Cebolleta. Two months into their patrols, the Diné have taken thousands of sheep from local ranches. The post commander sends dragoons to find and kill the Navajos. They ride the garrison horses into ruin looking for the Diné warriors. There is never a battle.

This all benefits certain people. Sandoval enjoys Cebolleta. He rides in with captives from his own people who are not his people. He sells a teenage boy for thirty dollars. On a day called the twentieth of March in a year called 1851, Sandoval rides in with eighteen slaves and many livestock. He brings several scalps.[39]

He is a man who is unashamed to be something no one understands. He befriends bands at Laguna Colorado, just over the Chuska Mountains. Then he betrays them. He takes their horses, the sheepskins they sleep on, the wives, the children. The Americans call him "our Navajo friend."[40]

It has been enough time. The Mexicans begin dreaming of Navajo obliteration. Manuel Chávez, the survivor of that slaving raid, who pulled Navajo arrows crosswise out of his body, has come to manhood. He speaks with the American governor and asks that he be allowed to raise six companies of militia with one hundred men in each company, to ride the war out to the Navajo. They ask for no pay. They will live on plunder. Chávez swears the militia will be in direct command of the governor, to be used at his will. The governor agrees and the American government officially sanctions Indian slavery for the next twenty years.

Edison runs down along the valleys of the frontage road. Water flows and summer trees hiss and sing along the concrete-lined acequia. Hummingbirds zip past Edison. Ducks call from the reeds of the ponds and small wetlands formed in the basins of dark lava rock along the road.

We follow the flow of the water.

The Acoma people saw the Long Walk unfold. They made friendships with the Navajos when they got back. It was easy to remember the old alliances. They traded bread and corn for Navajo mutton and wool. Edison came to Acoma with his mom and she was well known here. That trade tapered off in the 1970s, but it happened often before that. The Navajos would trade meat and wool for corn, squash, and bread. The Navajo *ato'* (mutton stew) is believed to have developed at Acoma.

"It was a delight," Edison says. "Like that calamari with that extra special spice."

The Acoma people always had more corn. Many Puebloan people will say Navajos are synonymous with movement and often acknowledged them as superior runners. In the Zuni way, Morning Star and Evening Star first offered corn to the people. Morning Star made a race to decide how they would divide the corn. The Zuni, Acoma, and Navajo offered up their fastest men.

The men ran. The Navajo man finished first, followed by the Acoma man, and then the Zuni. Morning Star breaks an ear of corn into three chunks. The Navajo got the tip, the Acoma won the middle, and the Zuni took the butt end. Evening Star told them, "It is well. The Navajo is the swiftest runner. He will always be moving from place to place. He will not be able to take care of much corn."

Even as Navajo men grew older, they would have special "old men" races.[41]

Edison runs with energy. He boxes, ducks, and jabs with the shadow cast by the Armada. He whoops up at the cliffs when he thinks he sees something threatening him. He is an old man. He is running.

A lone *naaĺeeĺí* (duck) swoops toward us and settles in one of the many pools of reeds and cattails in the black rocks.

We stop as the country opens up into a field with tall grass and a line of cottonwoods growing along a stream. Edison sits in the camping chair behind the Armada.

"I don't know, guys," he says. "I think if we just get a little trailer or a lift gate, attach it to the hitch, mount this chair on there, we can be in Santa Fe by tomorrow."

Everyone laughs. He looks at Lorraine's feet as Jason ties her shoes for her.

"Tie those shoosh," Edison jokes to himself.

He lifts his head. The fields and the cottonwoods spread green on the other side of the fence. A chestnut gelding with a white blaze stands unflinching, flicking his tail on the other side of the barbed-wire fence.

"You know, we could use that horse as our marker if he agrees to stay there," Edison says. He tents his fingers like he's just made some piercing business insight.

Joe Lunny calls for a group picture. Everyone says, "Cheese!" and "Achii!"

Edison says, "McDonalds."

He needs to go and eat. Jason ties the neon-pink marker and they drive away.

Col. Edwin Vose Sumner arrives in Santa Fé. The American government hemorrhages money to keep New Mexico. Sumner arrives to slow the bleeding. His plan is simple: to defend the towns from the Indians, move the forts out to where the Indians live and bring the pressure down. Sumner calls the headquarters at Santa Fé a "sink of vice and extravagance." He creates a new headquarters at Fort Union, on the other side of the mountains from Taos, near the community of Mora, far from any influence of the Mexicans. He soon learns this war has persisted as a result not of the Navajos but of the New Mexicans.

Sumner writes that the "New Mexicans are thoroughly debased and

A nest of turquoise robin's eggs on Mount Taylor. Photo by Jim Kristofic.

totally uncapable of self government, and there is no latent quality about them that can ever make them respectable. They have more Indian blood than Spanish, and in some respects are below the Pueblo Indians, for they are not as honest or as industrious."[42]

Sumner proves himself rather industrious. He rides a force of four companies of cavalry, one of artillery, and two of infantry ten days over 230 miles to a holy site at *Tsehootsooí* (Meadow Between the Rocks). Grass fed by springs rolls in waves of shimmering green between sandstone buttes. Sumner has his soldiers build an adobe mud and log fort at the mouth of a small canyon that shines with water. Maidenhair ferns sparkle in its light.

The Navajo are no longer devils living in a misty dream beyond the blue rise of mountains where they are the Lords of the Earth. The Americans are at their door. Sumner calls the place Fort Defiance.

The Diné begin calling the white Americans *Bilání joghal'ndi*. This gets shortened to the slang word *Bilaa'gaana*. It means They Are Many and Keep Coming.

This morning, National Public Radio reports on a couple who came to the hospital when it was time for the woman to give birth. They are married at the hospital bed by another pregnant woman waiting to give birth, who was anointed by the Universal Life Church.

Dr. George Tyndall—a gynecologist at the University of Southern California health clinic who faces several lawsuits for sexual harassment—was photographing his patients' genitals.

The NPR voice on the radio this morning asks, "How much should civilians monitor police behavior?" The story is about civilian oversight groups checking on police.

Since when are the police a military unit? Since when are citizens "civilians"?

A chestnut horse near Acoma, New Mexico. The horses often saved the people.
Photo by Jim Kristofic.

The answer is simple. The citizens have called themselves these names. It's all there in plain sight.

The power-seeking beings—call them Stephen Kearny, Manuel Armijo, Edwin Vose Sumner, George W. Bush, or Donald Trump—hand out the labels and the citizens strap them to their bodies and go on with their day.

I remember the first time I heard National Public Radio reporting on the economy and they stopped using the word "customer" and started using the word "consumer."

You shop at the grocery store? You pay a group of guys to rotate your tires? You subscribe to Netflix? You are a *consumer*.

You might have busted your ass through machinist school while waiting tables. You might mill gun barrels and fabricate tools most of the day. You might teach kids how to counter logical fallacies, how to research a problem, how to extend their thoughts into sentences in a public school. You might have put your face to books for eight years earning that biology master's degree so you could punch your card at a clean room laboratory where centrifuges spin blood and embryonic fluid for the production of childhood vaccines. But you are not a producer of anything.

You are a *consumer*. You are unworthy to take the levers of power. You cannot sit at the helm. And we have you. Come into the smoking circle. Everything will be fine. You will never see the knives. Not until we hide them in your bodies. Come and live in the paradise by the river. The cottonwoods are so shady and green. There is plenty of firewood. You can plant here. Come to the Round Forest. What a story. Who really believes this?

But for their sins, the people accept it. Who has the vision? Who will perish?

Say what you will about the consumer. Say what you will about the producer. But know this: no consumer can ever be a hero. And when people use that word across the airwaves, it is not an accident. But today, Edison is running.

I wake and crawl out of my sleeping bag in front of *Tsoodził*. The setting moon is orange and alive. The sky glows blue with dawn in the east. I make prayers and walk my dogs, Rainey and Ricky.

The blue mountain does not speak. It tells us the answer. The skull does not speak. We hear it, too.

If the United States is hemorrhaging money to bring New Mexico into the fold, then Fort Defiance becomes a compress to staunch the bleeding. Sumner writes on November 20, 1851: "This predatory war has been carried on for two hundred years, between the Mexicans and the Indians, quite time enough to prove that unless some change is made the war will be interminable. They steal women and children, and cattle, from each other, and in fact carry on the war, in all respects, like two Indian nations."

He appoints Major Electus Backus as commander of the fort. It becomes the most distant army post from Washington. Sumner understands there are really two visions of the war. One vision has already been fought, where civilian militias enter Navajo country, raid Navajo rancherías, kill what they can, and steal children as slaves. The other vision is where the civilian militias are kept out of the country and the army determines the peace. Sumner prefers the latter.

An American named Preston Beck puts in a request for arms through the civilian governor Calhoun. Calhoun thinks it's a great idea. This is the first vision of the war. Sumner agrees. He issues seventy-five flintlock muskets, cartridge boxes, bayonet scabbards, belts, and plate from Fort Union.

Sumner stipulates that the muskets cannot be used in forays into any Indian nation and can only be used when accompanied by military personnel. And they would be returned as soon as Sumner ordered it. This is vision number two.

Sumner understands that Beck is a scheming entrepreneur trying to keep the Indian conflict alive so that he can fleece the government while they occupy the territory. If you want to hear of men like Beck today, just turn on the radio. These raids are irrelevant to the war anyway. Sumner knows he controls the Navajos by their dearest possession. He arrives at Jémez on November 15 with Calhoun to negotiate a treaty. When the Navajo chieftains refuse it, Sumner cocks the hammer and promises he will find Navajo cornfields and rip them apart. The Navajos will not grow a single field of corn. He knows the Navajo can run and avoid his soldiers' patrols and expeditions. The *naadąą'* (corn plants) cannot. The chieftains understand this. Sumner has accomplished what the armies of Spain and Mexico had tried in vain for centuries.

Things seemed poised to go well. Many Americans see the Diné as the ideal Indian America was looking for or trying to create. An Indian agent at Jémez writes Calhoun: "These Indians are now what the U.S. government is striving to make of all the wild Indian tribes—a farming community."[43] This agent is appointed acting Superintendent of Indian Affairs when Calhoun leaves his sick bed, orders his coffin built, loads it on a wagon with his two daughters and their husbands, and joins a merchant train headed east for the States in the last week of May 1852. He dies on the trail and is buried in a town named Independence.

Sumner does not hold Sandoval in high regard. He says he is an "unprincipled scoundrel and it is plain that he has everything to gain by a war between the Navajos and the whites, for then he can steal from both sides."[44]

We meet at dawn and the chestnut horse with the white blaze is still there. I offer him red cabbage. He refuses. A slice of apple. He snorts and tosses his head. He will have none. He's an Acoma-grass kind of horse.

Everyone shows up. I meet Edison. He says hello as he walks into the run. We begin to move with him. He's taking it carefully this morning.

Edison dodges traffic in his run to the Sky City casino. We get past and keep down Route 66.

At the first stop, Edison reaches down and picks up a discarded branch. He starts limping with it as a staff, as a joke.

"He ran to Santa Fe and he became an old *chéí*," he rhymes. Everyone laughs.

Edison holds his water and says Joe should take a photo of him holding the staff. I say he looks like a song-and-dance participant. Lorraine says her mom used to love going to song and dance in Window Rock at Nakai Hall. Lorraine used to take her.

Edison dances two miles. Jason asks where they should find breakfast. Someone says McDonalds, back at the gas-station travel plaza across from the Sky City Casino.

"McDonalds?" asks Edison. "Fair enough. You know I've said this often to my kids. Mostly to my sons. I would say to them to establish your situation. Refine your professional skills. Make yourself a person who can relate to others in a professional manner. Build up something for yourself. Your resources. So you have something to draw upon. For vacation. A home. For helping your family. Even for dating. That way, when you take your woman to McDonalds someday, you can say, 'There it is, my dear. *Anything on the menu.*' And then we'd just laugh. I build it up like this serious thing. And then it's McDonalds. And anyone can just get anything. Because its *cheap.*"

Edison shakes the rattle. He runs into San Fidel. The ground on either side of the road is wretched from cattle. Only the cactuses have survived the war of the bovine maw. The grandkids dream of leaving this place. And many have.

This is a world made cheap.

That spring, five Navajo men from Black Eagle's band kill a rancher named Ramón Martín at Vallecitos. They take his eight-year-old son and his nephew and three shepherds. They hold them ransom for a paint horse and a mule. These five men push the army to move seven hundred troops into Navajo country. These troops will kill every man they meet. They will burn every cornfield they find.

Sumner says it will give him great pain to do this. But words mean nothing in this country. They fall to the ground and shatter.[45]

Sandoval becomes the international enemy. His own people want to get rid of him. He's an asshole. But he's the Americans' asshole. A captain under Sumner writes: "We ought to sustain him and use him as a scourge . . . the most effective rod in terrorism to be held over these people is the fear of permission being given to the Mexicans to make captives of the Navajos and retain them."[46]

The governor, William Carr Lane, wants to send in militia to settle the score. Sumner orders his troops to shoot any militia from the saddle. The governor challenges Sumner to a duel. Lane was elected nine times as mayor of St. Louis. Sumner shakes his head and refuses. Lane resigns.

People forget about Martín.

Edison stops and rests in the camp chair at Cubero. Cottonwood trees shade the concrete ruins of buildings.

Edison—the *jau̓di̓*—observes the devastation.

"Well, you all know what happens when Clint Eastwood comes to town."

Lorraine and Jason laugh as Edison takes a sip of his Sobé water and gets on the move. He is running east to Budville. The cottonwoods rattle.

After two miles, he rests in the chair.

"You know, I was telling Joe that if you dropped a hundred-dollar bill on the ground, I couldn't pick it up," he says. "I'd look at it. Shrug. That's nice. But I wouldn't get it. No way. It's the soreness."

He wets the bandana on his wrist. "This thing is a lifesaver. I was wondering a way that would best fit my needs. Wear around the neck? A headband? The whole bandana was actually too much. So I cut it in half."

The road continues through Cubero. And Budville. The only well-kept building is the Church of Latter-Day Saints.

Jason notices the only businesses still open are bars.

We stop to admire an abandoned trading post in Budville. Its Aermotor of Chicago windmill turns slowly in the gray, dead Siberian elms.

Edison steps into the last two miles to the intersection of the Khe San Bridge. Edison was in his teens when America slashed and burned into Southeast Asia. Two of his older brothers went to fight in Vietnam. Jason and Lorraine prepare to break for the morning. Edison sits in the shade.

"I need to eat and then sleep," Edison says. "I could eat that horse we met this morning."

Jason ties the neon-pink marker.

"I can't say what part of my body aches," Edison says. "All of it aches."

Henry Linn Dodge rides out to Navajo country as a lieutenant with the troops that cut apart Narbona's body with cannon fire. He becomes the agent to the Navajo at Fort Defiance. He travels the country more than he sits in his office. He is bad at filing reports. He is good at everything else.

He estimates the Navajos have 250,000 head of sheep and horses.

He rides into Santa Fé on August 31, 1853, with one hundred Navajo men. Zarcillos Largos, Manuelito, Ganado Mucho, and Armijo lead the column. The chieftains and their men carry lances and shields over their backs. Some have rifles across their saddles. They are the most feared men in America.

The women of Santa Fé call their children inside.

Nearly the whole town turns out for the ceremony the next day, where the governor presents medals to the chieftains. The governor gives Zarcillos Largos a cane to show that he is now the "head chief" of the Navajos. He and the other chieftains have no idea what this means. It is not in their character or beliefs.

After this trip, Dodge moves the agency east from the safety of the fort to the other side of the Chuska Mountains near the mountain pass where Col. Washington had set about his blood path four years ago, at a place called Sheep Springs. They say Dodge fell in love with a niece of Zarcillos Largos and married her in a traditional ceremony. But these are rumors. *Jíní. Jíní.*

By February 10, 1854, an army captain notices how New Mexicans are already grazing their sheep on Navajo lands. The ground begins to give way.

The mouths of horses and cattle work like shears upon the grass. The mouths of sheep work like a spear. They puncture the earth and take up the roots of the plant.

The sheep promise destruction for the ground. And all the while the Navajo find stories of how they were a gift from *Tłee'hona'éí* (The Moon Who Rules the Night). How they are a sacred animal.

The army captain estimates the Navajos' 250,000 head of sheep and 60,000 horses are already threatening to overgraze the land. He calls it "criminal recklessness."

That spring, Dodge rides in to Santa Fé with another group of Navajos. He asks for money for the Navajos to buy agricultural tools. He is denied.

He buys the tools with money from his own pocket. Men like Dodge still live on the Navajo Reservation today.

That afternoon, I travel to water. As I followed Edison running yesterday, I had seen this stream running pale blue over gray sand. Cattails emerge from edges shining green with algae. I wanted to come back. So now I am here.

The stream flows north beneath a bridge. Swallows dart from their nests beneath the steel girders of the bridge, oblivious to the strange symbols scrawled in spray paint that my kind would read as saying: "Leroy has a penis shaped like this." The penis done in black spray paint finishes in the shape of a horn, as from some bull painted in a cave at Lascaux in ice-age France. Next to the horned penis, someone has spray-painted: "Janie has a dirty pussy." What a fascinating culture.

The Diné met the Swallow People in the Second World, the Blue World. They called them *Táshchozhii*. The Spaniards that the Navajos drove from Cubero called them *golondrinas*.

Now a new world emerges where bats no longer find safety in the sunless dark. Temperatures we've unleashed by lifting the carbon from billions of tons of earth into the sky allow a white fungus to grow over the bats' eyes and faces and keep them from hibernating through the winter. They no longer live beneath the bridges.

But it appears *Táshchozhii* are making good on the promise of the First World. The mosquitoes fill the skies as the temperatures climb. The *Táshchozhii* swoop and flit to eat them and make more of themselves in the eternal hoop of their mud nests.

The stream waters run clear, with tinges of blue. It is the kind of water any Diné on the Long Walk would have drank.

The leaves fall gold from the cottonwoods along Black Creek and in the canyons. A Navajo man kills a soldier outside Fort Defiance.

The military says the soldier was ambushed. People later learn that the soldier picked a knife fight with the wrong man. Dodge and twenty-five soldiers track the Navajo man up the mountain. Dodge asks a local *naat'áanii* (chieftain) named Armijo to help him. Armijo doesn't understand why the Americans don't just ask for payment of livestock or horses to settle the blood debt. But he promises to catch the man in seven days. He tells Dodge he can take his own son as a hostage until he returns.

Armijo and his clansman hunt the man. Armijo's nephew chases the man up a slope. The man is ready. He puts thirty-eight arrows into the nephew's buffalo-hide shield before the nephew is able to fire and hit him in the side of his thigh. Dodge marches everyone back to the fort. Zarcillos Largos, who is the war chief, and one hundred other *naat'áanii* bear witness to the decision to hang the man until he is dead, dead, dead.[47]

The leaves fall gold from the cottonwoods along Black Creek and in the canyons. They cut the Navajo man down from the noose once he stops twitching.

Dodge hands out the tools he purchased in Santa Fé. They work. Dodge believes he can save the tribe from the raiding trail by sending the young men to the fields.

Perhaps he understands the corn song, the *tádídíín* in the ceremonies, the passing of light across the ripening melons. Perhaps he does not understand how the raiding trail has been a way to keep the Mexicans at bay and in check during a century's war of attrition. He might as well ask a mountain lion to become a farmer.

Dodge reports the Utes are trying to recruit the Navajo to abandon their fields this year and make war to drive Americans from the territory. That April, five men leave Abiquiú to Ute camps to sell them corn. The Utes take the corn and kill the Mexicans. No one ever recovers the Mexicans' intact bodies.

The Utes lose battles to the Americans. They attack Navajo *ricos* (rich men) living south of the San Juan River. They kill the men, steal the children, and run off a hundred horses.

The wars are a disruption to a plan Dodge can envision. He wants to see Diné people ride the storm of oncoming American settlement, not to be crushed by it. He writes: "A liberal and enlightened policy towards this tribe for a few years will fix their destiny as an agricultural, manufacturing, and stock raising community. That these results can be speedily attained by them no person will doubt who is acquainted with their habits of industry, temperance, and ingenuity."[48]

Dodge calls a council at modern-day Red Lake. Governor Meriwether and his son, his secretary, and two servants ride out from Santa Fé to attend. When they arrive, a *naat'áanii* named *Cach'osh Nez* (Tall Syphilis) yells at them and calls all Americans sonsabitches. Manuelito grabs him and pulls him outside. Tall Syphilis allows himself to be pulled. Both men have lost things.

The governor wants to talk borders. "If we have a dividing line so that we know what each other's country is, it will keep us at peace." The Americans do not know that the Diné believe their borders to have been born by mountains rising to the sky, by rivers cutting the rock. Their fantasy is the reality. American maps are the fantasy.

The *naat'áanii* go to talk together while their families trade, visit, horse-race, and gamble.

The next day, the governor awaits Zarcillos Largos. He does not appear. Instead, he sends in his medal and staff from the ceremony in Santa Fé nearly a year ago. They try to give the medal and staff to the thirty-seven-year-old Manuelito. He will not take them. They represent the power of the old man. They restring the medal and the governor gives over his own steel cane before Manuelito will accept.

They talk borders. Only one of the four sacred mountains is included in the borders.

W. W. H. Davis, the secretary accompanying the governor, is impressed with the Diné, with their "ingenious blankets," their strings of fine coral, their silver concho belts, how their horses ride with tack and saddles they have made. He notes how they "treat their women with more respect than any other tribe, and make companions of them instead of slaves. A Nabajo never sends his wife to saddle his horse, but does it himself. The modern doctrine of 'Women's rights' may be said to prevail among them to a liberal extent."

That summer, General Garland attacks the Utes. The Utes back down. The Navajo are able to pull a bountiful harvest. It will be the last for twenty years.[49]

I drive north up the juniper mesa to Acoma. The slaughter of the trees is obvious. If anyone doubts that we've broken down the climate, that droughts are myths, let them come here and see what myths can do.

The junipers are clawed to skeletons by drought-bred winds. More than one in five have died. You slowly climb the mesa. The skeletons pass you. The mesa opens into a broad cliff. You see for tens of miles to the east. Below are the mesas of Acoma. It's like coming up on a raw belief of survival in this desert. Giants of sandstone rise to the sky. And at the center of the monument sits Sky City. The Diné call it *Haak'oh*.

I meet Beverly Cisneros in the shade of a small city palacio behind the Haak'u Cultural Center. The groans of walking cattle fill the dusty air. Men and women whistle and call from their horses as they drive the herd south and west of the city. They have planted the fields with corn. So it is time to move the cattle. Tomorrow they will have their run to bless the seeds.

On Beverly's table sit beaded earrings, some plastic, some made with finer stones. Her pottery shines in white, painted with dyes made from yucca and sandstone. The symbols on these pots rival in age the iconography of the Spanish who tried to claim Acoma, but they're probably older.

The golden rim on the side and on the bottom of the pot represents the sun. The black triangular forms represent the mountains and the clouds. The straight lines represent the rain. Beverly paints these lines with fine brushes made from her granddaughter's baby hair.

Some pots are of the open style for holding water. Some are smaller, grapefruit-sized with only a small hole at the top and a small hole at the bottom. This is a seed pot. The small hole at the top keeps insects and mice out. It is just large enough to fit the seed. The hole at the bottom is just large enough to allow the seed to drop out for planting. The sandstone houses on the cliffs above are just large enough to house the people. And, yes, they *are* positioned at the top of the cliffs for defensive purposes. The Acoma people traded and farmed. But they had enemies. Everyone did.

Beverly was going to school to become a certified nursing assistant when her daughter—who was also going to school in Albuquerque—was hit by an SUV while crossing the city street. She was spared the bulk of the vehicle that would have bludgeoned her into that *baaschlizhiin*, that asphalt. Eeyah. Instead, the SUV swerved in the last minute and the large side mirror struck her in the head. Her brain was damaged mysteriously and likely forever.

Her daughter doesn't have the patience to work with the pottery. Now she does the beaded earrings and contemplates how objects and memories of the past are closer than they appear.

The sandstone walls of the homes in the village (which now host ten people year-round) are preserved by the adobe mud plaster applied to their faces every two or three years. The rain has become rare and the plasters are lasting longer these days. Some of the men who have worked the crews in the wider world have brought back with them the concrete stucco. They—like those men from Cubero—have grayed-over their grandfathers' work. Now they have more time for television or cruising in their Ford trucks or whatever else they do.

I drive back up the cliffs and walk Rainey and Ricky at the edge of the mesa overlooking the valley. Rainey sniffs at the ground. I see what she has seen. A fragment of a pot, white, lined with black for rain.

The Comanche join up with the Ute. They hit Manuelito's camp and steal his favorite horse. Manuelito chases them hundreds of miles into Utah territory. They have to give up, turn homeward, and the Comanches follow them back. They wound Manuelito and he drops into a fever. Zarcillos Largos prays and chants over him and gives him herbal medicines. Manuelito comes out of it, knowing that the Americans' promises for protection are now worth the sweat he has given to the ground over the past days.[50]

The year unfolds with threats and bravado over stolen sheep. Then come the fights over the grass. An army officer at Fort Defiance, Silas Kendrick, wants Manuelito off the grazing lands used by his grandfathers.

"Your army has horses and wagons, mules and many soldiers," Manuelito retorts. "They are capable of hauling in feed for their own livestock."

Kendrick threatens to drive him from the ground. Manuelito says he can call a thousand warriors around him in less than a day. Dodge knows that Fort Defiance is a skeleton affair. "They are no fools and see at a glance that the troops of this place are too few to prevent them killing and stealing."[51]

On October 18, 1856, the Santa Fé *Weekly Gazette* publishes an editorial claiming the Diné should have no grazing lands east of the Chuskas. The author is James Collins. He will become the Superintendent of Indian Affairs in New Mexico Territory.[52]

Dodge stands against this. He accompanies the Defiance post commander and a detachment of soldiers to the hill country south of Zuni. Dodge goes out hunting. Then he is hunted. Dodge's comrades think he's been kidnapped for some kind of ransom. A month and a half later, they learn from the brother of Mangus Coloradas that Apaches had shot Dodge with a carbine and left his body. They rode on to steal a flock of sheep at Laguna, cross the Río Puerco valley, and ride off another flock before descending to Gila Country.[53]

When Dodge's body has filled the bellies of crows, things change. The Utes get their confidence up. A Navajo man takes a new thing with him when he goes hunting: the fear that he will return home and find his wife with her head stove-in or his children stolen by Utes or New Mexicans or Puebloans to be sold in the markets of Santa Fé or Taos or into Mexico.

The world turns against them. The rains travel away. The cold freezes the soil deep enough to kill the roots of the peach trees.

The Navajo remember these years as *Naahonzood* (The Fearing Time). It was as though Americans had devised a weapon that could smash seven-tenths of a gram, the size of a peppercorn, of U-235, an unstable, rare breed of uranium, into another canister of rare uranium bred in centrifuges that could unleash the light of the suns and unfurl 20 kilotons of explosives that left people in ash piles and bleeding from within. It was as though then was today. *Naahonzood.* The Fearing Time.

The Aermotor windmill creaks in the cottonwoods as Edison steps into the run and dances two miles.

He rests in the camp chair. I tell him I've met people who know Andy Martínez, Edison's long-ago competitor from Acoma, who the women would adorn with necklaces, who would lay blankets over his back, who would give him the arrowhead that he would place in his mouth before he started the race that would end in his victory.

As a freshman, Andy Martínez ran a 4:10 mile. Edison, at his peak of training in college, could almost touch a 4:10, but he never broke it.

Edison rests after two miles. He shakes the rattle.

"Andy Martinez. He went to school right up there." He indicates a tall mesa. "He used to run that mesa. They had a cross-country meet every year. It would run up that mesa and then over to that water tank way over there. If you fell, you were done. It was so narrow. So rocky. And you couldn't pass. So you just had to pick your spot and follow."

Edison runs through New Laguna. People wave from their neat front yards. Rose bushes burn red and green against the adobe plaster of the small homes.

Edison stops to rest. His ripstop hat has developed a tear at the top.

"Careful with that," Edison jokes. "That's a K-Mart Blue Light Special." He did actually buy the hat at the K-Mart in Santa Fe. I ask how he found a K-Mart anywhere.

He smiles and steps into the next two miles into Laguna. We stop in the shade between a cut in soft-gray sandstone. Edison sits in the chair. Something smells sweet and fragrant in the air. Lorraine picks up the leaves and yellow flowers of a nearby plant and gives them a sniff.

"There was this group of Chinese educators who came to the Native American Prep School," Edison says. "They were there to explore the methods we were using. Really the methods that I used, to get the results we had. They arrived with interpreters and we'd be explaining things. When they were done, we had a beautiful dinner. At the end, they gave me a scarf, a silk sash. When someone noticed the scarf, they said, 'That is their highest honor.' So I rolled it up. I set it carefully in a box. And I never knew what happened to it. It's just gone. I think one of my kids must have it."

A car engine growls toward the gap in the road. A Dodge Charger with a steel grill guard stops suddenly and a Laguna Tribal Police officer gets out wearing a flak vest, handcuffs, a pistol mounted in a holster over his heart. He is Laguna, light-complected, with dark freckles under his eyes. He probably cannot run as fast as Edison.

He walks up with no slack in his pace. Rainey scrapes at the window, growls and rips like she wants him in her fangs. Rainey will lick a baby in the face. She will let a toddler jump on her and yank her ears for hours. But when she sees a cop, she will grant no quarter. Perhaps it is their way of walking, their propensity to cover their eyes with the strange black plastic lenses, that they must reek of metal and gunpowder.

So Rainey does her thing while the officer asks us what we're doing. I say we're doing a run. The cop looks through me. He doesn't want to hear from the white guy.

"That's right, we're doing a run to remember all those great runners," Edison says. "Andy Martínez. Gary Louis. Meldon Sánchez. All from Laguna and Acoma."

Edison does not make eye contact with the cop. The cop gets in the Charger and drives on.

I remark how Rainey never acts that aggressive to anyone but cops.

"Well, good," Lorraine says. "She's a good little girl."

"She knew him by his *chizhi* breath," Edison smiles.

Across the Río Grande stands *Dził̜iin,* the black mountain that holds the dark sorcery of atomic fission. The place reminds us of our deep betrayal by a military that promised peace in our time but instead gave us the constant fear of nuclear incineration. *Naahonzood.* The Fearing Time. Forever.

We get into the vehicles and drive on. For the dogs, the scent of gunpowder lingers in the air.

In January 1858, a war party of Utes crosses the Colorado River below the mouth of the San Juan and rides to Canyon de Chelly, where they kill a *naat'áanii* named Pelón. The Navajos complain to the major at Fort Defiance about the Utes who ride in under the army's noses. The major requests additional troops and claims the Navajos are growing "restless." The Navajo do not understand that the Americans are counting on the Utes to weaken the Navajo, just as they are counting on the Navajos to weaken the Utes. And when the dust has settled and the blood has soaked the ground, the bald eagles will descend for the carrion. Those eagles will grow fat.

A peculiar form of tax begins. New Mexicans approach the Americans. They claim stolen livestock with no evidence of their existence. The stock is stolen more than 150 miles from the lands of Zarcillos Largos and Manuelito. Yet the chieftains ride out and give livestock to Fort Defiance from their own people. And all to save from destruction the cornfields promising children who do not starve.

Manuelito will not move his herds from his grass and ground. The commander at Fort Defiance dismisses him and tells him he and his band are no longer friends of the Americans.

As Manuelito rides out, the commander orders his soldiers to walk out and shoot more than sixty of Manuelito's cattle.

The commander does not know how to react when a Navajo man walks into the fort a few days later and shoots his negro slave in the back.[54] Nobody can explain why he does this. There is a rumor that the man was insulted by a lover or a wife.

This man has two parts in him. There is a part that will seek harmony in the world and will connect to the everlasting life that is the destiny of every living thing. And there is a part of him that can never find harmony in the world. This spirit is that *ch'įįndii*—always hungry, always cold, always needing what cannot be found. It wants you to die. It cannot go into the spirit world and live forever. It is an idea.

What can we say of it? These dark things inside our minds.

The commander issues a simple order: bring in the murderer in two months or we burn the tribe. Sandoval—that man who is Navajo and who is not Navajo—hunts down the murderer and brings in the body of the killer. He asks for a wagon to bring in the corpse. The soldiers deny him and give him a blanket for him to carry the body.

Sandoval gives over the corpse. The post's assistant surgeon examines the body. He concludes that the body was freshly killed. The man was shot through the liver and lungs, probably while sleeping. Then someone walked up and shot him in the head. The Navajos say the man had been shot days ago and died of his own wounds. The corpse says he was shot just the night before. The man who shot the slave who belonged to the American commander was easily over forty years old. The corpse is of a boy no older than eighteen years. He is a Mexican slave. The Diné have traded one slave's life for another.[55]

The American army declares war.

Col. Miles leads an expedition the next day. They march to Canyon de Chelly. They will chastise the Diné into obedience.

They march and burn wheat and corn, the parts of the Navajo that cannot run away. They capture six thousand horses and sheep. They murder six men who stand their ground so their families can flee. They capture one man, six women, and children. They lose two men, and several are wounded.[56] Terror visits families and wives feel pain because one man feels pain from his wife and walks into the fort and visits terror on a black slave man who never knew freedom.

This is Navajo country.

A new commander takes over the department from General Garland. He enjoys the killing. Shooting buffalo is rare fun. For this new commander, men are the "nobler game" and the "retreat and slaughter and scalp were glorious."[57]

They ride out and attack the home of Zarcillos Largos. Six people die under gunfire near the houses. The Army captures fifty horses, buffalo robes, blankets, and saddles. They throw the possessions on a stack of wheat and burn it all. They march into the Chuska Valley and shoot ten people. They steal five thousand sheep and seventy-nine horses, burn *hoghans* and fields.[58] The troops gather in a final coup de grace against Canyon de Chelly. They recruit 160 Zuni warriors to ride to Ganado and assassinate Manuelito and his family.

Edison picks up a staff and walks in laughter. He becomes old for only moments. San Fidel, New Mexico. Photo by Jay-Lynn Bunion.

Someone catches word at the fort. They send a runner.

Manuelito and his people receive the runner. They flee and they make it. But the fields and their homes become ash. In the end, it is all a mission to nowhere. The columns of troops cover 350 miles to kill four Navajos, wound four others, capture and slaughter less than 350 sheep and cattle. The troops learn the lesson that must be relearned: the Diné are too intelligent to be lured into a decisive battle where all odds stand against them.[59] They put survival before glory.

⊹ DAY ELEVEN

I wake to the dawn and roll out of my sleeping bag in the back of the Prius. After dawn prayers, Rainey and Ricky and I walk the parking lot near Sky City Casino. I repack the car and go inside the nearby convenience store to get coffee. Outside, a large woman sets up a clipboard on a folding table. She tapes a poster to the table that reads: "Registration."

"Yá'át'ééh abíní," I say, and she and I converse. She is a staff member for the Navajo Nation Special Diabetes Program that is putting on a fourteen-day relay run for a "Stronger and Healthier Navajo Nation." The run is championed by Navajo Nation Vice President Jonathan Nez, from Shonto, Arizona, a church-attending Christian who runs often and advocates nutritious eating habits.

The "Running for Resilience" program had begun on May 14, four days before Edison left Spider Rock. It started at Bosque Redondo at Fort Sumner and the participants will run over 408 miles to Window Rock. The relay run is meant to promote diabetes prevention and

Edison looking north toward Mount Taylor behind Cebolleta Mesa.
Photo by Jim Kristofic.

awareness and to celebrate 2018, the 150th year of *Naaltsoos Sání* (the Treaty of 1868) that effectively ended the time of the Long Walk. The treaty returns to Navajo lands in a month, where it will be displayed at the Navajo Nation Museum before returning to Washington, DC.

I had asked Edison why he did not think to run from Fort Sumner back to Navajo country in order to deliver the Message. He did not feel it was appropriate.

"It was understood," he said. "The harshness of things made it so that you were not supposed to go back to that place. Because of what you might bring back with you. The ghosts. I actually thought it would be good for medicine men to go to Fort Sumner. I spoke with some of them. They are aware of how to fix things. Do a ceremony. Talk to what is there. Make a ceremony to fix it. They were not interested."

The vice president has said the run is "not a re-enactment." But many Navajo people are walking from Bosque Redondo and back to Window Rock. On some days, the path of the run extends more than thirty-five miles. Some days it's more than forty miles. Is anyone running that entire distance day after day? What are they bringing back with them?

Edison starts the morning run downhill to the east toward *To'hajiilee*, New Mexico. The country opens and the desert extends in bands of red and gray rock.

The crest of the Sandía Mountains emerges in pale blue. We are closer.

At the end of the twelve-mile morning run, Edison's older brother, Emerson, and his wife pull up in their Honda Element to celebrate the completion.

Jason mentions that we'll be stopping for a feast once we reach Santo Domingo pueblo.

Santo Domingo has a census of 3,500 people. Taos Pueblo has 1,600 members. Acoma Pueblo has 6,000 members. Laguna Pueblo has 7,700 members.

The Navajos have 350,000 people living on and off their lands.

Zarcillos Largos rides in with other *naat'áanii* to ask for peace. Armijo— one of the *naat'áanii*—brings his son. He stands the small boy in front of the soldiers. The wind blows the hair in front of his dirty face. A raven flies into a naked cottonwood tree.

Armijo asks the soldiers to see his boy. He will lose his son and so many more if the war continues. Can you imagine that today? The United States prepares to bomb a country. A leader from that country stands in front of Congress and he brings in his son and has him stand on the blue carpet in front of the C-SPAN cameras. He speaks the words Armijo speaks. Do the planes still fly? Do the bombs still fall?

One of Zarcillos Largos's wives walks in with a white flag.

The US government calls for a new boundary in the east that would steal all arable land and grazing land from the Diné people.

Bonneville and Collins ride out to Fort Defiance. They call the black-smith into the room. He is a Navajo man named Huero and he is a minor chieftain. Bonneville and Collins declare he is now the chief of the entire tribe. They have him sign a paper giving up all the fertile lands at Callitas, Bear Springs, Ojo Caliente, Red Lake, and in the Chuska and Tunicha valleys. We don't know what Huero thinks during this. He is coming up against a new force called American diplomacy. It is theft by paper.

Huero knew men who rode out on horses painted with clay in patterns of lightning, wearing the skins of lynx and mountain lion, who stole to feed people. You tell me which breed of theft has more valor. Historians call this paper the Bonneville Treaty.[60]

Zarcillos Largos knows his people can't keep the treaty. He calls for a *Naachid,* a meeting, to be held at *Tsin Sikaad* (Standing Tree), northeast of modern Chinle.[61] He directs the building of a ceremonial *hoghan* dug into the earth like a kiva. He chants for eight days while the fires of a thousand families flicker in the dark outside. On the ninth morning, the war leaders and peace leaders meet in a clearing. In the center, they pile their war moccasins, medicines, shields, lances, bows, and arrows.

Zarcillos Largos is remembered to have said, "I have seen this. I do not want to think of it, but it comes to me. Our sacred mountains were covered with black clouds, swirling in wind so not even the Great Ones could see the peaks. Throughout our valleys and across our mesas not one breathed or moved. All that broke the death silence from the tops of the mountains to the bottoms of the canyons was the howl of wolves and the wail of the black wind. Death."

Manuelito speaks. It is the Diné way. When a man insults or cheats you, you must put his head in the dust. Even if that head belongs to a gang who has walked into the country and defeated the Mexicans in less than a month. There is no real choice. Both sides want war over land and water. One will fight with bullets and—most importantly—a mobile supply chain of food and impoverished immigrants ready to replace the next fallen gang member. The other side will fight with arrows and the constant need to bury and hide any corn they can grow. This is decided at *Tsin Sikaad.* The decision will end in a thing called the Long Walk.[62]

In the afternoon run, Edison dances the miles two at a time. He feels this strange energy of anticipation.

He sips at water. Always the sips.

"There is that anticipation of leaving," he says. "You left Mount Taylor. That feeling transpired to loneliness at times. But it was that anticipation. That uncertainty."

Running east to Laguna. New Laguna, New Mexico. Photo by Jay Lynn Bunion.

He is mostly thinking of the details. He must make sure everything is happening as it was planned.

"There is a thinking of 'what will I need?' It's like getting ready for winter. All necessary to make it through. But I also know where I'm going. Very different for them during the Long Walk. Still, so much can go wrong here. I could get a blister so big that would just put me out of commission. So many things can go wrong. But they haven't. So far."

In the drive away from Edison, the chorus from that Tom Hall cowboy song cries out over the radio for faster horses, younger women, older whisky, more money.

Edison takes to the road from the Armada and Route 40 drifts beneath his pounding feet. The dance has begun. It all moves in those patient two-mile increments. The horizon drifts in mirages of heat. False ponds spread in reflected light across the black pavement. The sacred colors— white, blue, yellow, and black—are all there. They are running to the east. Edison dances after them until it is time to break for the morning. Jason ties the neon-pink marker beside the road.

The Utes keep killing. They ride down and kill at Abiquiú. Their agent, Albert W. Pfeiffer, knows this and tells no one.[63] Collins calls a council to stop the fighting. Sandoval—that Navajo who is not a Navajo—has died in the winter. By spring, some young Navajo warriors raid a Ute camp within three miles of Pfeiffer's agency at Abiquiú. A few days later, they ride into the homestead of Felipe Chávez. They are quiet. They come making the soft hooting of owls. The shepherds think they see a mountain lion in the distance, under the moonlight, stalking on the edge of the scrub oaks. One raises a lantern. The mountain lion is actually a man covered in a mountain lion skin. He draws his bow and shoots near the lantern. A Mexican drops from the saddle gurgling blood. The warriors take two thousand sheep and kill two more shepherds.

The Americans try offering another treaty. Zarcillos Largos is tired. His people give up livestock to the New Mexicans but they never see any return of their women and children who have been taken and baptized and serve as slaves at the houses, sweat shops, and ranches of Santa Fé and Albuquerque.[64]

The new Navajo agent takes a seventeen-day horse ride over the country. He estimates the Navajo population between twelve and fifteen thousand. They have large herds of horses, sheep, and goats. An American captain who joins the trip writes that a war against the Navajo "would fall heaviest upon the least guilty—would transform a nation which has already made considerable progress in civilized arts into a race of beggars, vagabonds, and robbers."[65]

Edison runs with the dreams of Acoma. Photo by Jay-Lynn Bunion.

It is all the same: sprawling gangs of criminals called governments pulling people into the furnace to smelt a thing called Power.

The Mormons see the trend and try to unite all the tribes between the Río Grande and the Colorado River. They tell the Navajo they are being cheated out of their land. Ganado Mucho and his family spend most of the year riding between the Colorado River and the Chuskas collecting livestock. They see it as a kind of perverse tax to protect their corn to keep the soldiers away.

Perhaps it is all summarized in one day.

Fort Defiance gets a new commander, a captain, Oliver Shepherd. That autumn, he assigns an escort to the agent Silas Kendrick, who will take livestock given by Ganado Mucho's family back to Albuquerque. The first night out, a group of Navajo men stampede the herd and get away with eighteen horses. This does not help things.

The next morning, a man rides into the camp and gives over two army rifles he says he found. This man is a relative of Ganado Mucho. The army lieutenant with Kendrick suspects the man of stampeding the livestock. He orders that to keep the soldiers away from his family, the man must take the rifles to the post to Captain Shepherd. He also gives the man a piece of paper. But the man feels the energy of the situation. He rides to Ganado Mucho's camp and asks the *naat'áanii* for his advice. Ganado Mucho tells him to take in the rifles and the piece of paper.

The man reports to the captain. The captain takes the rifles and decides the man has taken too long to arrive. He has soldiers grab him. They take his shirt. They tie him to a wagon. They whip him until his back bleeds.

Someone sends a runner. Ganado Mucho hears of the whipping. He washes his hands of the Americans. Kendrick is also angry. He writes: "Such treatment as this is what destroys all confidence of the Indians in the poisonous justice or common humanity of government officials."

He says Ganado Mucho was "one of the most faithful and efficient friends of the whites in the whole tribe."[66]

But no more.

The small valley of the passing Río Puerco opens before Edison. The Route 66 casino shimmers on the south side of the freeway. The highway screams. The glass and steel cut the air. The heat billows through the trough of sand and sagebrush. Billboards read: "Stay and Play."

His body handles these things in a quiet ceremony inherited over the millennia: sweat to expel the heat, then balance the salt and water, throw the blood to the skin to push out the heat or to the guts to pull energy out of the intestine or to the fats stored in the body.

Edison doesn't have much fat to spare.

Edison sips water. The dance continues.

By winter, Manuelito leads an attack of two hundred warriors against Fort Defiance's hay camp. They burn everything. Later, they kill four soldiers out collecting firewood.

Three miles from the fort, they attack the lumber camp and kill a soldier. Manuelito tries to cut the supply lines, but reinforcements arrive with better rifles.[67] Some Navajos try to make peace. Agua Chiquito rides into the fort and strikes up a conversation with Kendrick. Shepherd interrupts and demands words with the chieftain. Agua Chiquito ignores the captain.

Shepherd tells Kendrick that he is in charge and Kendrick can't talk to Navajos without his permission. Shepherd barks for the chieftain to leave. Agua Chiquito walks to his horse, disgusted. As he walks, Shepherd orders two of his soldiers to shoot Agua Chiquito. He runs. The soldiers start shooting. The bullets fly past the chieftain's hair. He makes an arroyo under fire and he runs away and any hopes of peace go with him.[68]

Kendrick travels back East.

The American Army has 1,800 men at its disposal. By January, a Navajo war party attacks the cattle guard of 44 men and they fight for two hours. The Navajos continue to hit supply wagons. They raid villages on the Río Grande. They burn ranches. They run livestock back east on their secret trails of vengeance.[69]

The New Mexicans want to handle the problem with militias, but the new American commander, Col. Thomas T. Fauntleroy, won't give them guns. He knows the dream is dead. Sumner created his Fort Defiance to issue threats and create a better world. Instead, many Navajos are punished for the actions of the few, government agents get murdered, and messengers are flogged. The Americans shake their rattle of power and expect the Navajos to quietly farm in awe. Instead the Navajos burn ranches.

Fauntleroy retreats the base of operations fifty miles east to Ojo del Oso and names it "Fort Fauntleroy."

Mural depicting *Jóhonaa'éí* (The Sun) over *Diné Bikéyáh* (Navajo Country) on a cinder-block utility shed at the local gas company. Artist unknown. Chinle, Arizona. Photo by Jim Kristofic.

It has been hard to sleep in the hotel room. But Edison returns to the neon-pink marker the next morning. Dawn is coming. The cool air massages his thin legs.

They call it the Nine Mile Hill and it opens before Edison into the valley of Albuquerque—*Be'eldíílasinil* (Where the Big Bells Ring). It is a place built for the automobile, where the land is carved into precise rectangles of concrete. It is not a place for runners.

Edison runs down to it. His cartilage accepts the concrete.

The hard surface is not what Edison likes, but his body has been trained to handle it. The pounding gives back to the body. When the foot strikes the ground, the heel and Achilles tendon stretch. As the foot rebounds off the toes, it sends 40 percent of the energy back into the body for the next stride. The arch of the foot additionally springs 70 percent of the impact energy back into the body.[70]

Edison does not think of this right now. It's getting harder to do math.

A Navajo warrior wearing a war cap made from the scalp of a mountain lion. Painting by Douglas Yazzie.

The highway screams and cars roar past. The heat drums. The dance continues.

Most of the troops ride or march out of Fort Defiance that April. Manuelito plans an attack and, within a week, Navajo warriors stalk over the frozen mud to the walls of Fort Defiance. Then they are firing in the blue dark at the three soldiers posted at the southwest corner of the fort. They surround the fort on three sides. Six hundred warriors pinch in from the east and west. They rush the walls. Soldiers fire, but the warriors take cover at the woodpiles near the garden. They take control of the outer buildings. They get into the storehouse and take most of the food. The 138 soldiers left behind at the fort get a better view within an hour as the sun rises. They are able to shoot eight men before the warriors fade into the pines. Some soldiers pursue, but they are called back when they nearly shoot each other in the dim light.[71]

The army calls for a winter campaign against the warriors. But New Mexico citizens don't want to wait. Superintendent Collins orders Albert Pfeiffer and Christopher "Kit" Carson—the agents to the Utes— to urge the Utes to make war parties against the Navajo. By the middle of May, four hundred New Mexicans and Utes take the war trail and burn *hoghans* and destroy fields in the ponderosa pines and meadows of Tunicha valley. The Utes guide the militia into the mountains and they get thirty-five children and kill six men and one woman.[72]

New Mexicans and Ute raiders later ride out from Abiquiú to hit the Chuska valley. Many of these men are the genízaros—those hard-living peasants of mixed blood, hungry to take their place in the world. Someone sends a runner. The Diné learn this. The chieftains make plans.

When the New Mexicans ride into the mountain pass, they don't see the logs and boulders perched at the edges of cliffs. It is all a pinch again. Warriors fire arrows and muskets at the New Mexicans from the front and rear to box them in. As the New Mexicans and genízaros and Utes try to escape up the slopes, the Navajo roll the logs and boulders on them. Horses scream. Men are crushed. Cartilage separates from bone. Dirt mashes into bleeding wounds and dry aspen leaves quiver in the mussed hair of corpses.

Fifty men rode out from Abiquiú. Ten ride back.

Can you see that warrior? Riding home after that attack? Imagine that man, walking to the fire. Leaves are in his hair. He takes off his helmet made of a mountain lion scalp. How long did he stalk that lion? How did he outsmart it to take its courage and prowess on his own skin? Who hears his war songs? Who hears his prayers? Who understands his bond to the Monster Slayer? To the Child Born of Water? Whose cornfield did he use to gather the pollen to make his blessings? Who gave him the white corn he used to make his dawn prayers? What is his name? Where does he place his war helmet of lion skin? Does he worry his children will find it? Does he worry that mice will eat the hide while it sits up on a shelf in the *hoghan* somewhere? Does he wonder if he might never see the future? How do his muscles feel? Is he sweating? Is he exhilarated? He has put four men under the earth. He walks out and squats. His shit makes steam in the oaks and he kicks leaves over it.

This is a man who will take a bow and ride into bullets.

He breathes in the night. He crushes sand in his fist. He contemplates things. He knows he will need to have the Enemy Way, where he will be cleaned of the ghosts of the men he has killed. He must also have his own dark nature calmed after it has risen up to help him kill his enemies.

I have shown you something you will never see in an American film: a Diné man who has killed European men and now sits in contemplation of their death. He participates in a thing called introspection. The fire paints shadows on his face. The sand runs out of his hand.

He does this. But he is not allowed this. He is a savage. So he must whoop and dance with a bloody scalp at the end of his lance. He is not allowed sorrow. He is not allowed pain. He is not allowed grief or pity or ambiguity or fatigue or fear. These things would make him human.

This warrior is not permitted to worry about his children or his parents. Only white settlers may do this, and they must do this most vehemently when they hear this warrior whooping and crying at the edge of the light through the glass window of their log cabin.

Men from Abiquiú and Taos—many of them genízaros—begin to sing of this man and his people. They sing in Spanish:

Heya, he weya, he yaha,
Ena heyana heya ha.
If you go to Navajoland,
If you go to Navajo, yes.
If you go to Navajoland,
Take your shroud,
Because death over there
Is firm and without doubt.[73]

Who is this man?

No American tongue could say his name. That tongue would fall to ashes.

Where is this man now?

He is running.

He is running with Edison.

The pounding continues. The pounding. Edison feels it. He does not speak much. He wheezes at the smoke born of the oil fields. The miles come. Like a required suffering, they come. In this Place of the Big Bells, the suffering is free to all.

Fauntleroy hands off the Navajo assault to a colonel named Canby. Three columns of soldiers will fan out from the Río Grande. They will murder and burn until the women come walking into their camps with white flags asking for peace.[74]

Canby leaves Abiquiú with 138 troops and five times that number of Puebloan fighters and eight times that number of New Mexican militia men and genízaros follow behind the Americans to swallow livestock and the dreams of children.

Canby knows these men are merely slavers and he doesn't want them. But the government must win the hearts and minds of the locals. So they go. He meets another column at Canyon de Chelly. They spend the month of October marching their horses to exhaustion. They encounter no Navajo warriors. They kill five horse herdsmen on Black Mesa. But they do find camps and over a hundred Diné women and children go to the markets in Santa Fé and Taos.[75] Utes attack from the north. They take as many and capture thousands of sheep, horses, and cattle. But no one finds the men who attacked Fort Defiance.

But someone finds Zarcillos Largos. He visits the Hopi to build alliances. He rides back past Sagebrush Spring south of Klagetoh and runs into a slaving gang of New Mexicans partnered up with Zuni men. One of the men knows Zarcillos Largos and tries to warn him. It is too late. The New Mexicans fire. Zarcillos Largos fires from his horse and kills four. He turns his horse to ride away but the horse is shot out from under him. He takes cover behind his dying horse. He shoots until his arrows are gone.

His attackers close in and shoot him until he convulses with arrows. They break his arms with rocks. They break his legs. This way, his ghost will not follow them back to Zuni and murder them at night. The Zuni cut his limbs open. They slice away his sinews from his bones. They wrap them up and return them to their pueblo to use as war medicine. The crows and coyotes have the rest of him.

The fields are abandoned. Ripe corn rots. Melons cook to mush. The Americans find no warriors. But they have won. The crops are dead. The winter comes.

Canby calls a treaty. He knows the Diné are more victims than boogeymen. They must be at peace with the New Mexicans. This thing called peace will be used to make a thing called progress that will give birth to Power.

Twelve days after some chieftains sign the treaty, thirty-one Mexicans from Taos show up at Fort Fauntleroy at Bear Springs. They tow four Navajo women by the neck with ropes. They'd killed one man, six women, and six children to get these four women. The slavers are starving.

Canby gives them food from the post provisions as a "matter of humanity."

Canby forces them to give over the four women. The men from Taos say they will defy the treaty and organize a new group once they get back. That group's job will be murder and slavery. The American soldiers watch them ride east to the Río Grande.[76]

The black rattle shakes and shakes. It is a comfort. It takes it. It takes it. It takes the pain.

Two Navajos are killed openly in Cubero. Two army scouts who are Navajo are shot at near Jémez. One is killed and scalped. By March, New Mexicans have attacked fifteen Navajo ranches in the Tunicha Mountains.

The Americans have been in the country for less than twenty years and they have already tipped the scales against the Diné.

Manuelito rides his cattle down to Fort Defiance. He grazes the herd inside the walls. The animals eat what is left of the garden where other Navajo warriors had taken shelter behind the woodpile and exchanged arrows for lead bullets less than a year ago. The ground is his. For now.

It is hard to track Edison now. The Armada must pull into a succession of church parking lots and car dealerships to give him water, to check the tape on his toenails, to wet his red bandana on his wrist, to apply the Chap Stick to his lips, to make sure he eats.

Always he stands. Always there is the rattle.

The decision for the war in the spring of 1861 is simple. Some southern ranchers from Texas join up with some influential New Mexicans and declare Arizona and the southern half of New Mexico as the Confederate Territory of Arizona.

The Navajos do not know this when they come to Bear Springs to trade. That September, people are running horse races. Manuelito falls into a special race with a lieutenant from one of the New Mexico militia. Many army soldiers have been called back to fight in the East. The army hires New Mexico militia to fill the gaps in their ranks. They put them in American uniforms and give them American rifles to guard Fort Fauntleroy. The Navajos bring their bows and their women and their children.

People lay money, blankets, jewelry, livestock, clothing, and food provisions into the gambling pool. During the race, Manuelito veers off the track. He stops his mount and finds the bridle slashed. The soldiers demand the lieutenant won fairly and they form a victory parade and march into the fort to get their winnings.

This moment will tell you something about the Navajo rage.

These people had hunted Mexicans to death. They had been hunted. Some of their relatives had been killed. Their children sold to slavery. The soldiers lock the gate. The Navajos shout at them. One of the men tries to force his way through the gate. The soldier at the gate shoots him. And the blood is loosed.

Go seek out "The Flood" by Robert Frost. Read that poem. In the time required to read that poem, fifteen people are murdered outside Fort Fauntleroy.

The Diné run in all directions. The soldiers chase them. They shoot them. They bayonet them in the back. A captain pulls together twenty men to stop the violence. They march out. The captain yells at a soldier standing over two children and a woman, about to spear them with his bayonet. He orders the man to stop. The soldier stabs the two children to death and nearly kills the woman. The captain grabs him and orders the other soldiers to take off the man's belts and imprison him.

Here is where we meet Chávez again. He is a shapeshifter and now wears the skin of an American soldier. They call him a colonel now. He is the post commander. He can count more than two hundred relatives killed by Navajos and other Apaches.

What do you think he does next?

He calls up the howitzer and orders it fired. The people are running. The shells explode over them and shrapnel pops through their bodies. Twenty people run no more forever.

The American captain hauls the New Mexican soldier to the nearby New Mexican lieutenant and explains why he disarmed the man. The lieutenant pulls his pistol and screams, "Give this soldier back his arms, or else I'll shoot you, God damn you!"

The captain puts the guns back in the soldier's hands. He reports this to Colonel Chávez. Chávez says the lieutenant "did perfectly right" and that the New Mexican soldier who had murdered the children deserved good "credit" and not criticism.

The bodies lay on the cold ground. But was Chávez really there to see them? He was at Bear Springs. But was he in the same time? Or was he still walking dead from that ambush when he was a teenager, with seven arrows in his body and watching that Navajo boy die? Had he still just buried his brother? Where is he now? Perhaps he is now merely a glimmer of light reflecting from those lines of ordnance depots in that ground, at what is now called Fort Wingate, where bombs and artillery shells sleep and hiss beneath the earth.

I wait for Edison, Jason, Lorraine, and Jay-Lynn outside the Lavato's Trading Post at Santo Domingo Pueblo. The tribe changed its name to the traditional Kewa Pueblo about seven years ago. It was a unanimous decision among the council.

The white walls of the church shine in the noon light. This was the place where Oñate passed sentence on the rebels at Acoma, where he made their men either slaves or cripples.

Today, two kids—one eight years old and the other probably fifteen—walk through the heat, each carrying a plastic bag filled with twin two-liter sodas. A child runs ahead of his pre-teen sister, waving a Spider-Man action figure. He yells, "Spider-Man!" as he runs to the door of the trading post.

Edison arrives. I say I have brought him something. I point to the Prius.

Three paw prints stand out in mud against the metal hood. They are bear tracks. They are as big as my hand. I live in the Valdez Valley, where the Rocky Mountains ascend over a mile into the air from the Río Hondo. On the night I returned to Taos, a bear climbed up the front of the car. *Shash* did not break off any windshield wipers. *Shash* did not dent any of the metal. *Shash* likely leaned onto the roof and smelled the inside of the car. Or he gave a blessing. *Shash* drug his hand over the rear taillight. *Shash*—whose moccasins are black obsidian—bent the edge of my yellow New Mexico license plate to show he had been there.

They say that bears' paws are very greasy. The grease has kept the prints intact, despite the drive over more than two hundred miles of highway.

"That's a blessing from the Taos mountains," I say. "Mountain medicine."

Edison quietly nods his head. "Oh wow."

Within six months, Fort Fauntleroy will be abandoned.

Many of these men would ride to meet the Confederate army invading from Texas. Canby will strike no more treaties with the Diné. He is now leading that army.

It is confusing. The tribe of Americans have now split in two. The men in the blue uniforms wilt in the fighting because the Texans shoot back and do not allow themselves to be bayoneted. They are not families of women and children, trying to defend their cornfields.

But the Confederates soon have their supply wagons burned to ash by a Colorado force a third their number. They learn they are on ground that does not tolerate the European way of war. Columns of men fall to starvation and thirst before cannon and lead slugs can rip their bodies.

When the Confederate threat is gone, the New Mexicans go back to slaving. Each captive easily sells for four hundred dollars in Santa Fé.

The slaving becomes so noticeable in 1862 that Dr. Louis Kennon, a longtime Santa Fé resident, writes that the Spanish excursions are all exercises in theft. Dr. Kennon knows "no family which can raise one hundred and fifty dollars, but what purchases a Navajo slave, and many families own four or five, the trade in them being as regular as the trade in pigs and sheep."

Before the War, these slaves cost seventy-five to one hundred dollars. Kennon also believes the Indian Bureau and military have encouraged slaving since the beginning of the Civil War.

Six thousand people live in Santa Fé. At least five hundred of them are Indian slaves.[77]

One of Ray Lovato's relatives meets us at the trading post and guides us down the tight dirt roads between mud-plastered houses to Ray's place.

Ray Lovato walks out of his squat, concrete-stuccoed house. He stands bowlegged in his gray and black plaid shirt and jeans. He balances himself on his woodpile next to a rusting skeleton of one of the many broken-down trucks in his dirt yard. His bracelet shines with three turquoise stones. I will learn this bracelet is worth over $3,500.

He sees me in the Prius and points next to the wood pile.

"Park here or they'll tow you," he laughs.

Rainey and Ricky settle in.

We enter the cool shade of the house and Ray's daughters and nieces give us all the side-hugs common to Kewa Pueblo. Beneath the dark vigas and plank ceiling, a long table shines with bread from Ray's *horno*, sweet potatoes, ham, chicken-salad sandwiches, watermelon, cookies baked in the *horno*, potato salad, and so many sugared drinks I can hardly count them all.

Edison starts drinking punch and eating ham and potato salad right away.

Ray's father built this house in 1956. The beams and boards are dark with stain. Cleanly finished mud walls move the cool air into the room. Paintings done by a local man hang under where the pine vigas meet the mud wall. Images of mule deer, mountains, and Bob Marley.

Edison shakes the black rattle and explains he's using it to honor the Apache who were also at Fort Sumner. He offers it to Ray and his family. They shake it. Edison explains it was made for him many years ago by a Jicarilla Apache.

"It sounds almost as good as mine," Ray says. "I should let you use it."

Ray brings out his rattle, made from an orange gourd. It really does sound great. Edison smiles and nods with excitement. Ray holds out a white gourd. He says he's going to make one from that gourd.

Edison motions to Ray's daughters and nieces and nephews. "Please, please, join us," he says. "I'm full. I'm a runner. We can't eat much."

Ray scratches behind his short ponytail—his *ponsai,* as they say at Taos Pueblo. He asks Edison if he still has his number for ordering more jewelry this year.

"I have, like, five numbers for you," Edison says.

"What? I only gave you one number," Ray says. "I have the other five numbers for my girlfriends."

Edison and Ray laugh with everyone else.

Ray's granddaughter brings out a small display tray full of loop earrings of turquoise and white shell. Jason bites deep into a slice of watermelon. The ham is sweet and so perfect.

Edison jokes to Ray's granddaughter, "Set one aside for me, huh?" He winks as though he's just worked a secret deal.

"Did I show you my long-strand necklaces?" Ray asks.

Edison shakes his head. "Not the recent ones."

Ray parades them in. Beautiful turquoise nuggets spaced with white shell. They sell for three thousand dollars each.

"Not a lot of people do long strand anymore," he sighs. "Sometimes the word just has to get out, and the people find you. I had a man come here to visit me one time. A British guy. He was here. His young wife. Their four little girls. We visited. We cooked and ate. We talked music. He and his wife and all the kids bought long strand. He had big money. I think I have a picture of them here somewhere."

Ray shuffles into the kitchen. Lorraine dishes out more potato salad.

Ray walks back with the picture. There they are. All smiling with the turquoise necklaces. The wife. The four little girls. The British guy. He is Eric Clapton.

If you want to get down, you've got to take her out. Cocaine.

Everyone smiles in amazement and passes the photograph.

Ray shows Edison his big strand necklace. It is tied with sinew and has massive turquoise nuggets the size of eagle eggs. One strand is made by his late son. He'll never sell it.

It is important to show everyone hospitality and to be generous. Some people take advantage of Ray's traditional generosity. "I can't be Santa Claus every day," he says.

Ray begins to joke. Ray jokes about his bracelet and how everyone who meets him wants to buy it. But he doesn't sell. He'll keep it until they cut his arm off.

He jokes about how a customer once asked him if he worked with "Sleeping Beauty" turquoise. He said, "No, but I have Wake Up Ugly!"

He walks into the kitchen and comes back holding a mug shaped like a large breast of a white woman.

"This is what I drink out of," he says. "It's why I'm so happy!"

Ray's daughter Marsha walks in wearing a yellow and red T-shirt from last year's Red Ribbon run. She tells of the many relays they do with the Jémez Pueblo for the state fair. They even have runners join them from Hopi. Her sisters tease Marsha because she promotes health and diabetes prevention while she is also at least fifty pounds overweight and may become diabetic.

"Yeah, she's a *runner*," her sister says. "She needs to run!" And she claps Marsha's belly. It makes a crack like someone has just smacked the ass of a horse. Everyone laughs. There's no offense taken and no shame felt.

"She's got all the energy reserves," Edison jokes. "She's got what she needs! She won't have to stop running!"

"Yep," says Marsha, "I've got all these energy reserves." She smiles and shakes her gut.

Ray and Marsha reflect on the Pueblo relay run that the people organized in 1980 for the three hundredth anniversary of the Pueblo Revolt against the Spanish. Edison gave gear, shoes, equipment to one of the relay runs from Taos. But he kept it at a distance because it was a Pueblo matter.

"I hope this run moves forward with the spirit that will keep us bonded," Edison says. "It goes together. The rattle. It all fits in the same kind of hand. We are united. It is an honor to go forward with this message, with your blessings on behalf of the pueblos."

"This message," Edison says, rising from the table, "all comes from the heart."

Edison offers Ray and his daughters money for the food. But they refuse it. They say to save the money for a motel for the run. Edison offers Ray a buckskin medicine bag with corn pollen inside. He accepts this.

Edison walks slowly to the Armada. He collapses into the leather seat. The pounding of the pavement haunts his knees and ankles.

"There have been times when I've been at Indian market, where Ray has his beautiful work set out in three jewelry cases," he says. "I'll walk up to say hello. And he'll cover the jewelry cases with these black cloths and we'll sit behind his table and share a meal. Just to talk. Just to discuss things. And I tell him, 'Ray, every second at that market is worth a *lot*. You should keep your jewelry displayed.' But he always shakes his head. Or when he's been at Hubbell. First there is the bread. The meal. We eat. We talk. Then we trade or buy. That's the old way. Very traditional."

In late summer, General James Carleton and his 1,500 California volunteers arrive in New Mexico after recapturing Tucson from the Confederates. Carleton marches the Californians out to Fort Union, where Carleton is given command. It is a special honor. His mentor at the Pennsylvania Cavalry School had been Edwin Vose Sumner, the architect of Fort Union.

The Diné are out of luck. The Confederates are defeated. The 1,500 volunteers have no enemy to fight. The Diné will become that enemy. Also, Carleton believes there is gold hiding in Navajo country. Now the Diné are doomed.

Carleton knows the ground here well enough to know that it murders people. Each cornfield and peach tree is a sacred, green marvel. He will burn them all. He hands the torch to Christopher Carson.

So his operations against the free Indians in New Mexico will be simple: Pen them. Give them Jesus. Look the other way. The place for penning these "wolves of the mountains" will be a small cottonwood forest in a desolate country on the Pecos River. Here, the cottonwoods grow in a ring. Locals call it Bosque Redondo—The Round Forest.

Carleton argues it is a good location because it is far from white settlement. He fails to note that the Navajos' own country is already far from white settlement. A board of army officers assigned to inspect Bosque Redondo knows that the place will fail. They write that it is "remote from the depot supplies, Fort Union, and from the neighborhoods that supply forage. Building materials will have to be brought from a great distance. The water of the Pecos contains much unhealthy mineral matter. A large part of the surrounding valley is subject to inundations by spring floods."[78] They recommend a site near Las Vegas, New Mexico. But Carleton is the general. The fort goes up on the Pecos and he names it in honor of his mentor: Fort Sumner.

In the meantime, the slaving parties ride out from the Río Grande. Navajo children vanish and reappear as baptized Catholics in the households of Albuquerque and Santa Fé. It is a dark magic.

This afternoon, Edison is running. It is hard to track him around the Jiffy Lube, the Target, the Starbucks, the Pizza Hut. I cannot help but think about the old Navajo woman who guided Edison to the high school in Torreón. No cattle guards, telephone poles, and fences here. We are back to taking lefts at the credit unions and taking rights after the diners.

Edison sits in the camp chair after the Armada pulls into a hotel parking lot. He takes water. He tries not to talk too much.

"I'm too old for this," he says.

"You're not too old for this because you *are doing this*," Joe says. He snaps some photos.

The Sandía mountain stretches seventeen miles across the eastern horizon. *Dziłjiin* (Jémez Mountains) stretch ninety miles across to the east opening of the Jémez country, where twenty-one chieftains once walked into the smoking ring—into the round forest—and had their hosts stab knives into their hearts. To the north, the Rocky Mountains run into the country of the Utes and the boundary of the sacred mountain of the East—*Sisnaajini* (Where the Black Line Extends—Mount Blanca).

I tell Edison this is a special place for mountains.

In this world, mountains are born three ways. There is the slip-fault mountain, where the massive tectonic plates push on each other and drive one edge of the plate up and over the other, like how the ocean forms a wave. Sandía Peak is a slip-fault mountain. The second type is the collision-fault mountain, where the tectonic plates smash into one another and push their edges into the sky. The Rocky Mountains are collision-fault mountains. The third type is the volcanic, where molten metal and ash meet the cold sky and form the dark slopes. The Jémez Mountains are volcanic mountains.

There is only one place in the world where you can see all three mountain types at the same time. And it is here. We are in that place.

"Beautiful," Edison says. "That's cool!"

Then he is running. The light drops to the golden hour. The blood-light strikes the slopes of the Sandía mountains. The moon looks down like a silver eye.

We stop after two miles. Edison has to switch shoes.

He pushes on the toe where his blister tape has come loose. The toenail flexes and looks like it's going to fall off. If Edison squeezes hard, it will fall away like dead skin.

"That's a disobedient little toe there," he says.

He slips his feet back into the cushy blue and white Nikes he'd worn at Canyon de Chelly. He steps into the next two miles, up and down the pavement. The pounding. The traffic screams. The lights turn red and green. The cars flash past and the cool light of cellphones glows from the dashboards. It is a different kind of world not made for runners.

The Californians hit the Mescalero Apaches before the Navajo. Carson learns early that these California volunteers have a bloodthirst. He advises a Mescalero chieftain named Manuelito to ride to Santa Fé to see Carleton in person and ask for peace. The old Apache chieftain tries to surrender his band. They ride. On the way, they meet a group of American soldiers who do not know of Carson's advice. Six men and a woman are shot on sight. The soldiers kill five more. Carson is disgusted.[79]

He meets a large group of Mescaleros at Fort Stanton who ask for his protection. Their Chief Cadete says, "You are stronger than we. We have fought you as long as we had rifles and powder; but your weapons are better than ours. Give us weapons and turn us loose, and we will fight you again; but now we are worn out; we have no more heart; we have no provisions, no means to live; your troops are everywhere, our springs and waterholes are either occupied or overlooked by your young men. You have driven us from our last and best stronghold, and we have no more heart. Do with us as may seem good to you, but do not forget that we are men and braves."[80]

These words speak today.

Over four hundred men, women, and children go to prison at Fort Sumner in March 1863. Edison remembers them. That is why he runs with the rattle. It is made by Apache. Jicarilla band. It is a comfort. The gourd is painted black. The color of the North. Of death. Of reverence. Of return.

Edison is running. The Armada pulls into a church parking lot and Edison rests. He soaks the hat. His back is a country of sweat.

"That was the hardest mile," he says.

He won't take water. He can feel his belly expanding. His right ankle is starting to harm him. He rotates it.

"They had great pain. Suffering," he says. "I'm feeling every piece of it. With every step I take."

He watches the Sandía crest. The last strips of the blood-light—that gold and crimson color—streak the edges of the peaks.

"I wonder if it was worth it," he says.

"What?" Lorraine asks.

"The whole thing," he says.

The sunset light strikes the shield of the crest.

"It's beautiful," he says.

I know Edison is seeing Sandía Peak. He is also seeing *Dził Nááyisí* above *Be'eldíílasinil* (Where the Big Bells Ring).

But he is also seeing something else because his mind and body are in a place all of ours are not.

"I'm in a trance right now. I can only feel half of what's going on," he says. He feels this as we approach the parking lot of the Goodwill in Rio Rancho. Scientists and sports trainers call this "being in the flow." His oxygen level. His heart rate. It is all somewhere else.

He runs until he reaches the junction between Route 313 and state Route 550 in Bernalillo, New Mexico. This is where Jason ties the neon-pink marker to the post next to the Giant gas station.

Edison sits in the Armada and Lorraine drives him to go and rest.

The Diné watch this war against their Apache cousins. They know they are next. Chieftains called Barboncito and Delgadito ride out to Fort Fauntleroy and meet with Carleton to strike a deal for peace. Carleton hammers out his words: the Navajo will join the Apaches in the round forest in the desert.

Barboncito tells the California general that he will not fight the Americans. But he will also not go. "I will never leave my country, not even if it means I will be killed."

Carleton understands his own answer. On May 10, 1863, he writes to General Henry W. Halleck. He wants to "brush back the Indians" so that "the people could get out of the valley of the Río Grande, and not only possess themselves of the arable lands in other parts of the territory, but, if the country contained veins and deposits of precious metals, they might be found."[81]

He writes again a few days later: "There is evidence that a country as rich if not richer in mineral wealth than California, extends from the Río Grande, northwestwardly, all the way across to Washoe (Nevada)."

A month later he writes to Captain J. G. Walker: "If I can help others to a fortune, it will afford me not quite as much happiness as finding one myself, it is true—but nearly as much. My luck has always been not to be at the right place at the right time for fortunes."

In that letter, the Diné share some common ground with the general.

The Europeans need space to come to the ground and dig it apart to find their fortune. For the Diné, the ground was their fortune. That is what you need to know.

Edison rests after running the seven-mile hill leading to the edge of the Albuquerque valley, where the Nine Mile Hill descends into the city. Photo by Jason Bunion.

⊹ DAY FOURTEEN

Edison steps out of the Armada and lifts each leg. Tenderly. But he has good energy. Emerson—Edison's older brother—made them a good dinner the night before. Brisket. Pork chops. Mashed potatoes.

"We got into the wrong sport!" he laughs.

I suggest curling. Jason and Lorraine laugh with Edison. He walks into the morning run along Route 313 from Bernalillo. The Jémez Mountains loom to the northwest, that nest of volcanic violence and atomic witchcraft. Eeyah. Dooda. Edison has run more than ninety miles from where John Boomer celebrated his fiftieth year in Navajo country and spoke of the ghosts of uranium pluming up from the groundwater to be here, the destination in the dark mountain, where all that uranium was bound to go.

Edison stops to sip some Sobé water. The Avia shoes are working well. But they won't last.

Edison runs the pavement of Albuquerque—*Be'eldíílasinil* (Where the Big Bells Ring)—under the moon. Photo by Jim Kristofic.

The mountains of Santa Fé stand gray in the distance. He runs past adobe houses going back to earth next to faux adobes. The old world is still strong enough to stand next to this modern one.

We pass a Honda CRV. Its bumper sticker reads, "Don't Believe Everything You Think."

Carleton has a vision: The only peace for the Diné will come if they give up being "nomads."

They would live on the reservation and "little by little, the Navajos would become a happy, contented people, and Navajo wars would be remembered only as something that belongs entirely to the past."[82]

The vision is simple. For their bodies to live, their souls must die. The Diné must become the Americans that now live in Bernalillo, where Edison is running. And many have. They drive Ford or Chevy trucks, drink Pepsi, watch reality television, eat food they do not cook, and cheer for the Steelers or the Broncos or the Cowboys. Twenty percent more of them die of heart disease than other Americans. Nearly a fifth of all Native Americans have kidneys scarred and pancreases imploded. More than half of them beat or rape their women, punch their kids, or think alcohol is medicine. They are on the path to join the sixteen million Americans who have major depression, the forty-four thousand who commit suicide, and the forty million Americans who suffer sleep disorders. Americans no longer fear being killed by Indians. Now the Americans kill themselves.

A thousand men march out of Los Pinos on July 1, 1863, under Christopher Carson to help bring us this world.

The Diné have twenty days to surrender. The Americans will move out more like hunting parties than columns of soldiers. They will function much like the tribes they are attempting to exterminate. Many volunteers know this is a last chance to make a quick dollar on slaves. Once the Navajo make it to Fort Sumner, the market will close. Following in the army's wake are Utes, Pueblos, Apaches, Kiowas, and Comanches, ready to get what they can from the ruins of the Navajo families.

Carson—who was the agent to the Utes at Fort Garland—urges his Ute guides to take Navajo captives as rewards. He does this because he believes the captives will be better off being sold by the Utes to Mexican families who will care for them. Carson thinks going to the Round Forest in the desert will be worse.[83]

But he also believes that it will serve to break up their tribal identity. Or taking them to Bosque Redondo will throw the Lords of the Earth into a crucible of suffering that will only sharpen and harden them tighter as a people. There, the tribe may become unkillable. Carson is right.

Edison worries about the afternoon run.

"I can run the hills," he says. "It's the downhill that just kills me."

The miles roll out beneath his feet until Edison has covered over fourteen of them.

"We need to go get breakfast," he says.

Jason ties the neon-pink marker to the barbed-wire fence. He steps into the Armada, and Jason and Lorraine and Jay-Lynn drive him to the nearest diner to eat and then to their hotel to rest.

Edison is forty-four miles from Santa Fé.

I look to Sandía Peak and take the road to the east side of the mountain. The sagebrush and sand give way to green grass and aspen and pine as I drive over a mile into the sky to the Sandía Crest. I take out my binoculars and glass the country that Edison has run. *Tsoodził* looms blue over a hundred and twenty miles of distance. Rainey and Ricky and I walk the ridge to the north. Three red-tailed hawks sail overhead, two parents teaching a young one to scout the land.

To the north, a dome of white cloud blooms in the sky. Rain on the horizon. Or a cloud from a massive forest fire. It has been dry. It is too far away to tell.

I say hello to an elderly man who had hiked up to Sandía Crest from the bottom this morning. He grew up in southeast Utah and we swap stories of the beauties of the Manti-La Sal forest, where his father used to mine for gold and other precious metals.

"You ever heard of Mount Tukuhnikivatz?" he asks.

"No," I say.

"Well, that's the reason I went to college," he says.

I tell him why I am here, why I'm following Edison.

He smiles and says he'd worked with Navajo people at his father's mines. "They were such cool people. So cool."

The campaign begins. Nothing spectacular happens. It will be a war against plants and fields. In late July, Carson moves his command to Fort Defiance and renames it Fort Canby. Most of the Diné are already gone. They fled along the San Juan, to the wild country north of Monument Valley—a country labeled on American maps as Broken and Mountainous. But most move west, beyond Hopi country, some as far as the Grand Canyon and to the area around Navajo Mountain. The Diné knew the soldiers were coming. Someone sent a runner.

Carson sends out troops under a major to bring in all livestock and burn all fields in the canyon behind Fort Defiance. The Diné watch the corn become flames. One Navajo man leaves his hiding place in rage. He rides down with this pistol cocked and shoots the major out of the saddle. When the soldiers find the major's dead body, they discover he carries $4,300 in cash under his coat. No one knows why.[84]

A few nights later, some Diné men sneak into the corral at Fort Defiance and steal Carson's favorite horse.

This stops nothing. The *naadąą'* (corn) and *dibé* (sheep) and *nazísí* (squash) cannot run. By the first week of September, only fifty-one Navajo people had been sent to Bosque Redondo. Carleton gives an order to say every Navajo man must die.

"Say to them—go to Bosque Redondo, or we will pursue and destroy you. We will not make peace with you on any other terms . . . This war shall be pursued until you cease to exist or move. There can be no other talk on the subject."[85]

Carleton invites miners into the region to search for the gold hiding in the earth. He asks for more cavalry to protect the miners. "Providence has indeed blessed us," he writes. "The gold lies here at our feet to be had by the mere picking of it up!"

This is a lie. There is no gold.

The autumn comes. Manuelito and Ganado Mucho see the way. They begin fighting the long defeat. The war comes. The elders die first. Then the children. You have just killed your past and your future.

They have their bands pack the food. The grandmothers help the grandchildren to the country west of the Hopi villages. They follow the Pueblo Colorado wash to the Little Colorado River and to the confluence to the Grand Canyon. The cottonwoods turn yellow. The winds carry the leaves to the sands. The Diné watch their world change. The corn has ripened. Carson has his troops march in a line from Fort Defiance to Canyon de Chelly. They find few people. This frustrates the killers.

The horses often saved them. The animals can smell the leather and gunpowder on the wind. The Diné always had to flee from enemies. The corn patches were destroyed. Horses hardly ate much when the Diné were attacked. The horses heard sounds of approaching enemies. They would come running back to the camp with their heads held high. The people saw this. They fled.[86]

One patrol sees a *łįį ligai* (white horse) watching them from a mesa. A soldier kicks his mount and gallops up the steep slope. The white horse sniffs the wind and touches noses with the soldier's mount. The soldier cocks his pistol and shoots the white horse through the head.[87]

Watch for that white horse. When he runs, you run, too.

I drive to the marker tape near Algodones. NPR interviews an official from the US Navy about the difficulties in recruiting people. The official says 70 percent of high school graduates are unfit to serve. But they are hoping their new ad campaign will appeal to the young. They call it "Forged by the Sea." I am not sure if the official knows that forges involve fire and that his metaphor might be slightly mixed. It makes me question what percentage of people in the navy are fit to serve.

The radio announces that all forests are closed today as of 8:00 a.m. There is great concern of a forest fire. People smoking in the dry grass or running chainsaws among the dry groves of pine can send embers or sparks that create towering infernos. So the people are forbidden to walk among the trees. The deer. The turkey. The elk. These can be trusted. People cannot.

We return to the marking tape at Algodones. Edison steps carefully out of the Armada.

I have the sense that we are making up lost time. Edison is going to try to make fifteen miles tonight to put himself on a strong schedule. He wants to get to the base of the tall hill before he stops for the day.

"We're just going to go a bit at a time. Just take it easy," he says.

This means Edison will still run faster than over 80 percent of the high school students in Albuquerque. He starts forward and the dance begins for the evening. His form holds. His arms do not cross the center line of his body. The K-Mart hat is holding on. His blue The Message T-shirt flaps in the wind.

We stop after two miles. The hot wind races across the blacktop of Interstate 25.

He takes the water. "Don't go. I have to keep telling my body: don't go."

I ask if he feels his body is going to give out on him.

"No, I'm telling it not to go too fast," he says.

At this point, his body is well-rehearsed to create distance. He goes another two. The sun drapes the dry ground in purple light.

He stops. He sits and takes water in the shade of the Armada's canopy.

"They paraded Navajos in Santa Fe," he says. "The Americans. The Mexicans. They could have taken them to Albuquerque and then down to Fort Sumner. But they marched them up all the way to the capital. Kit Carson and those soldiers. So they could say, 'Look what we did.' As a *trophy*. They paraded them through the downtown. To the plaza. 'Look what *we* did. Aren't we so great.'"

He stops and listens to the scream of the traffic.

"Part of me just wants to have this done. They're going to say, 'Oh, what does this guy know?' But if I'm the guy who runs 330 miles. Oh. Then we should listen. It will give me that substantial . . . ah . . ." He laughs. "Credibility . . . or whatever."

Lorraine smiles sadly. Edison's tongue is in his cheek, but just enough to let the truth shine out.

He runs another two. We stop. Edison takes the chair. He sits, asks Jay-Lynn for Chap Stick. She takes his hat off to wet it.

"Sure, just take it right off. Take it right off me," he says. "Well, 'I'm Navajo, too.'" Everyone laughs at this inside joke.

"Did I tell you the story with that one?" he asks Lorraine.

"Yes," she smiles.

I ask him about it.

"Well, it takes a while to get into. But simply said my sister, Irene, is a manager at Lowe's grocery store in Gallup. And one day there was ... ah ... a *conflict,* shall we say, in the store over a woman being discriminated or prejudiced against. And they called my sister over to deal with it. And during the argument with the woman, my sister said, 'Well, I'm Navajo, too.' And everyone just started laughing."

"She has such interesting stories, Irene," Edison says. "As you know, Navajo people are still very traditional. You see it in Ganado all the time. They know lightning is very powerful. You do not mess with that. Eeyah. One afternoon there was this strong storm that moved over Gallup. It made lightning over the hills. Eeyah. And all the people are inside while they hear this huge lightning strike. The parking lot is totally empty except for one older gentleman who was just standing out there next to his car with his groceries, getting rained on. And what had happened was that a lightning had struck a pole near the parking lot, and all that energy drove down and dispersed through the water, and it froze him. It stunned him, that man. And with 90 percent or more of the workers at Lowe's being Navajo, none of them wanted to go out in the lightning. So they found a Mexican guy and said, 'Hey! Go out and help him!' And he was able to shake the gentleman and get him into his car before the ambulance came and checked on him."

Edison goes another two miles and another two. Another two. The mountains glow with yellow evening twilight.

In August, four Diné men ride up to Fort Defiance under flag of truce to negotiate surrender of their one hundred relatives. The major left in charge by Carson imprisons the men, then puts them to work burying shit from the outhouse and a few dead dogs left at the fort. Then they shoot one of the men. Two other men jump the wall. They run. They make the trees and escape. They keep running and carry a message about what it means to surrender to the Americans.

Carson has the major dismissed from the army. Nearly half of

Carson's officers on the expedition will be either court-martialed or forced to resign. They will be charged with murder, alcoholism, embezzlement, sexual deviation, desertion, and incompetence. One of his lieutenants is caught having sex with an enlisted man. Another lieutenant will describe himself as the "damdest best pimp in New Mexico" after he proves adept at finding prostitutes for his men in Santa Fé.[88]

Diné chieftains like Ganado Mucho knew two voices spoke to our actions. Our living spirit. And our *ch'įįndii*. If they had known these officers, they would know what voice spoke the loudest.

The runners go out. They spread the word.

The Diné perhaps know that they are being hunted by demons.

The soldiers take the corn, the wheat, and burn it. By November, the soldiers have destroyed two million pounds of food. A chieftain named Delgadito surrenders his people. Carleton wants to use him to bring people in. He gives his people special treatment, the beef with the most fat. Delgadito eats. He takes the suggestion to travel to Fort Fauntleroy and give speeches. Come to the forest. Eat. Be here. Or starve and freeze on the run in your own country. Free.[89]

If the soldiers find you, they shoot you. Often you are found by a small band of Utes and Ute scouts riding with Carson. If your baby cries, the soldiers come and kill you all. So you smother the baby. When the soldiers leave, you put the baby away to the earth. Very well. Stay here. We will find each other later. There are other worlds than these.

The American president ultimately responsible for the orders to hunt these families does not know it is happening. Not really. He is of the wet, green world of the East, and he visits a small village in Gettysburg, Pennsylvania, in those same weeks to speak at a site of a great battle and to dedicate a cemetery for the many dead. He says little, but people remember some of his words:

> The world will little note nor long remember what we say here, but it can never forget what they did here. It is for us, the living, rather, to be dedicated to the unfinished work which they who have fought here have thus far so nobly advanced. It is rather for

us to be here dedicated to the great task remaining before us—that from these honored dead we take increased devotion to that cause for which they gave the last full measure of devotion; that we here highly resolve that these dead shall not have died in vain.

And so Edison is running.

Edison drinks Sobé water.

"I'm just making no sense right now," he says. "I can't think. I'm making no sense, like I'm the President of the Navajo Nation."

I tell him nineteen candidates are running this year.

"Nineteen?! Wow! Russell better watch his back."

He says he should run for Navajo Nation president. I tell him he'd have my vote.

"I'd make a great president," Edison says. "'I'll take your wives. I'll take your money. I'll be a *real* big shot.' That would be my campaign slogan. I could just be honest from the start. And there would be people who would actually vote for me!"

Joe says, "Don't forget to pardon your crony friends."

"Yeah! Yeah! I'll do that, too!"

It is hard to pinpoint when Navajo leadership turned from an emergence of competent lords pushed forward by their own fighting prowess and diplomacy skills to now become a chain of well-dressed thieves. But I am sure that written laws had something to do with it. As did money. Before the Long Walk, if a group didn't want to follow their *naat'áanii,* they said, "To Hell with you! We'll go our own way!"

After the Long Walk, the Navajo adapted and, like the weaving they learned from the Puebloans and the horses they absorbed from the Spanish, the Navajo took in these *naaltsos'íí*—laws and charters from the Americans. They must be powerful medicine. The Americans had defeated them, after all. But even the first Americans feared this medicine was a toxin in masquerade. Thomas Jefferson noted this before the close of the eighteenth century when he published *Notes on the State of Virginia* in 1785. He wondered whether the dead might enslave the living by paper and ink. He wrote: "Were it made a question, whether no law, as among the savage Americans, or too much law, as among the civilized Europeans, submits man to the greatest evil, one who has seen both conditions of existence would pronounce it to be the last: and that the sheep are happier of themselves, than under care of the wolves. It will be said, that great societies cannot exist without government. The Savages therefore break them into small ones."

I would wager my Prius that no one on the Navajo tribal council has read this book.

Edison walks forward into the next two miles. He is limping for the first time.

I watch his stride as he runs. His ankle appears bent inward. I think I am seeing things.

He runs past the billboard advertising the latest band to play at Buffalo Thunder Resort and Casino: Blood, Sweat, and Tears.

Is Edison imbued with these faculties of a *naat'áanii?* Is he a *naat'áanii?* Well, he *is* running. And we are following him.

The run ends with Edison checking his toes. He has taped his pinky and the next toe on his left foot. The inside of his big toe is taped. He adds tape to the inside of his right-side big toe before lacing up. His toenails are taped so they don't fall out. Lorraine kneels in the shoulder to cut and tape his feet.

A helicopter flies overhead. "Uh-oh. They spotted us," Jason says.

Underneath the helicopter reads: Police.

Someone sends a runner. Barboncito and his band hide in their own country around Canyon de Chelly. They hear Carson has assembled pack mules to walk supplies in with his invading army. Barboncito's warriors sneak down into the corrals of Fort Defiance and drive Carson's mule herd into the dark. Carson sends troops after them, but a snow storm swoops down. The dark sky and thick flakes help the warriors escape with the mules. The mules disappear into the people's stomachs. So they can keep running.

Carson wants to delay the assault. General Carleton gives orders that the men can walk into the canyon carrying their blankets and four days' rations in their haversacks. A month later, the first column of three hundred men ride for six days over forty miles to Canyon de Chelly. Twenty-seven pack animals die from exhaustion in the deep snow. Pfeiffer marches to the eastern end of Canyon del Muerto.

The Diné waited at a place called *Lidbáásiláhí* (Smoke Signal Hills), where people moved into caves to hide from enemies. The people living here are the first to see the covered wagons of the army come down into the country. They do not know what they are. Some think the white canvas tops of the wagons are big snowballs in the distance.

The wagons come to *Dzil'ghaahas Kaí'í* (Apache Trail) toward sunset. The people with the wagons make camp at *Hóótsohgii* (Thunderbird Lodge today). The Diné see these are American soldiers and Mexicans. They have Navajo captives with them. These captives led the soldiers to the hidden caves. The enemies fire with rifles. The people fight back with bows and arrows. People scream as they are shot and fall from the cliffs.

Men fall from the cliff. Women fall from the cliffs while holding their babies. The babies who survive the falls cry at the bottom of the caves.

The leader of the American enemies sees all this. It frightens him. He breaks down and weeps.

He sobs, "What a terrible thing we have done to these people!"

The army rides back to their camp at *Hóótsohgii*. The commander still regrets what they have done. He sends two captives with a white flag to see if the people will stop fighting and surrender.

The captives walk up the hill toward the caves and say, "From here on we will not kill any more people or harm them in any way. I invite them to our camp and they are welcome."

Three men, all of them *Mą'ii' Deshgiizhnii* (Coyote Pass) clan, and one other man walk to the enemy camp, along with the captives who escorted them. They find tents arranged in rows, side by side. The soldiers spring out and point guns at them. The captives lead the four men toward a large tent where the leader waits. When the Navajos and enemy leader confront each other, they exchange greetings. Once more, the leader of the enemy breaks down and cries over the murders of women and children.

The men wonder, "If this leader is such a crybaby, why is he waging war out here?"[90]

151

Pfeiffer leads a hundred men down into the canyon. They find Navajo families running away. They fire into them. The men turn and die for their people. Two women and two children go into shackles.

The horses and the soldiers wade through two-foot-deep snow. Anything that can feed or house a Navajo child gets put to the torch. Any sheep or goats are shot. The Americans burn through this "Gibraltar of the Navajoes." The Navajos cry vengeance from the edges of the canyon like the mountain lions whose scalps and skins they wore when riding against the Mexicans.

Three men walk out of the night carrying a white cloth. They ask to surrender their families. Carson gives them until ten o'clock the next morning. The sixty Navajo people show up early the next day. The soldiers can count their rib bones through the holes in their clothing. Carson shakes his head. He asks why they had not just surrendered sooner. The families say that people had tried, but they were shot. They believe it is a war of extermination.[91]

Carson explains it is not. He fears he is wrong.

The next day, three hundred soldiers walk out to destroy a cornfield. It takes them the whole day.

Five thousand peach trees line the waters of Canyon de Chelly. They vanish to the ax and the flame.

Twenty-three more people are shot and killed. Thirty-four go into shackles. Two hundred people surrender. Who knows the names of those twenty-three people? Did they try to avenge the deaths of what had been theirs? Did they try to defend something the soldiers came to take?

By February, seven hundred Navajos have surrendered to Fort Fauntleroy.

Within two weeks, over a thousand camp outside the walls of Fort Defiance.

Edison wants to keep running. But it is time to stop. An owl has flapped through the purple dusk. We are at the Santa Fe county line.

"That's a messenger," Edison says.

"Is it a bad thing?" I ask.

Running past a casino billboard that advertises the band, Blood, Sweat, and Tears.
Photo by Jim Kristofic.

"Depends on who uses it," he says. "Okay, *shí buddy*. We'll see you in the morning."

He says something else, but I can't hear it. The traffic screams past.

He limps to the Armada and fields a call about needing to be at the house. And then he needs to leave right away to sleep.

I drive to a friend's house in Placitas and fall asleep in a guest bedroom with the wind smacking the window. The smell of fire mists out into the night. I wake to the full moon orange in the east.

The morning of the final day. The sun rises through pink haze. The mountains that were once the home country of the Jicarilla Apache are on fire. The news is calling it the Ute Park Fire. I saw it from the top of the Sandía Crest yesterday. Today the cloud of smoke looks like an A-bomb detonated in the pines near Cimarron, New Mexico.

Swallows hunt the cool air. Each beat of their fin-like wings is a mourning for the bats.

Two red-tailed hawks watch the Armada from their perch on a power pole.

Here it comes. That big hill up from Río Gallisteo. Edison is going to run a half-marathon this morning. Most of it will be uphill. He'll do another half-marathon at noon. Lorraine pours the water on his red bandana on his wrist.

"This thing," he says, patting the bandana. "This thing has been the lifesaver from the start."

He stretches his legs against the concrete barrier.

"That's the first time I've seen him stretching," Jason says.

"I know!" Edison smiles and laughs. "I'm always saying, 'Why are those guys even stretching!?' Now here I am doing it. All right. Let's go for it."

Edison runs uphill into the sun. I cannot see him through the windshield. It is all too brilliant to look at. Running north into the dawn. The last dawn. Jason and Lorraine have written with soap marker on the back window of the Prius. It reads: "The Long Walk. 150 years. The Message. The Run. Eskeets. 330 miles." The right-side window reads: "The Message. The Run. Eskeets. Hubbell Trading. The Long Walk. 330 miles." The left-side window reads: "Honoring the Long Walk. 150 Years."

Edison runs the hill in the dawn.

He is feathered in light.

The snow makes mud in *Woneeschííd* (The Month of Crying Eagles) when the first Navajo people walk east. One thousand, four hundred and forty-three people walk east out of Fort Fauntleroy with 473 horses and 3,000 sheep.

Ten people die on the three-hundred-mile walk. Three children are kidnapped by New Mexicans posing as soldiers.

These are the lucky ones.

The soldiers give flour to the Navajos who surrender. The Navajo women do not know how to cook it, and no one tells them. They make a kind of gruel—like they would prepare corn mush—that gives them dysentery. Over a hundred people die.

A week later, a group of 2,400 people walk out of Fort Defiance. The ones who eat the gruel on the walk bend with cramps and cannot go on. They are shot by soldiers. The old people who cannot keep up are given a little food. Then their families walk away sobbing. They are leaving them in the cold spring weather with freezing temperatures after sundown. The nights make you die. The soldiers shoot nearly two hundred people. Or they leave them to die in the desert.[92]

On March 20, another 800 people leave Fort Defiance and join up with 146 other people along the way. A snowstorm hits them for four days and nearly kills half of them. They make it to Los Pinos, below Albuquerque. The walkers camp in the open. During the pause, New Mexicans sneak into the camp and steal several children. An officer writes that Americans "will have to exercise extreme vigilance, or the Indians' children will be stolen from them and sold."[93]

By July 1864, nearly 5,900 Navajos live at Bosque Redondo. The soldiers hold another thousand people at Fort Defiance.

No one living today saw the walk. Neither does the man who commands it. General James Carleton stays in his quarters reminiscing of the Navajo as a valiant and heroic people who cannot withstand "the insatiable progress" of the Anglo-Saxon race.

He issues his order from Santa Fé.

Santa Fé emerges in shrouds of smoke. The message is on the horizon. More than a thousand Texans and New Mexicans flee their enclave at 7,400 feet elevation at Ute Park amid the aspen and pine groves while flames reach out brighter than any angel's fire. The people fear their wealth is consumed. Their investments pop and sparks fly upward. Edison's feet drum the asphalt. His heart pounds. The sun blinds us. This is not a metaphor. This is not divine retribution. It is happening.

He stops for water. Then he is moving. He runs past the Oñate Military Complex for the New Mexico National Guard. At the gate it reads: "A Legacy of Honor."

A soldier runs in his brown T-shirt, camo pants, and combat boots on the parallel frontage road. He is muscular and likely in his early twenties. Edison turned fifty-nine years old yesterday. Edison passes him.

Carleton unleashed the troops from Santa Fé. They found a Navajo camp? Burn it. They found a woman? Take her. A Navajo man? Kill him. A Navajo boy? Kill him. Nits make lice. Imagine how few heroes made the Long Walk. They had likely died months before, leading soldiers away from their families, giving their lives to give their wives those extra hundreds of yards from the shackles of the Americans. Young men died protecting their fathers. They were the Aeneases and Hectors of their day. Only no one knows their names. No one bothered to ask them. There was no surviving Aeschylus, no Ovid, no Virgil to record their drama, their comedy, their tragedy. The Diné have no Homer.

It is Treaty Day. This means something to Diné people, but it is not clear what it means to everyone. Some Diné have no written language to memorialize or warp their sense of reality. One of the first preparations a civilization makes as it enters its death spiral is to create a past for itself where it was once the oppressed who have now redeemed themselves. Virgil called into being the downtrodden diaspora that became Rome in *The Aeneid* when Rome had already bartered away its Republic heroism for land and imperial power. Thomas Paine and Thomas Jefferson trumpeted America as a rebirth of the Roman republic even as it champed at the bit to cross the Appalachians and steal lands from the democratic tribes in the Ohio River Valley.

One such landowner held title to ten thousand acres of land in this valley. When the war was over and he was able to parcel it out and sell it, he became the richest man in America. This man was George Washington.

The Navajo are telling their story of oppression. Only that story is still being told. It's not even a story. It's their lives. Don't believe me? Talk to Manuel Chávez. Talk to John Washington. Talk to James Carleton. Ask them for an apology. Ask them to resign. Let me know when they get back to you.

The chieftains in the tribe—like Manuelio, Barboncito, and Ganado Mucho—send runners. They run to the Round Forest. They run back. They bring the same message: to stay away.

Bosque Redondo becomes an open-air prison. It resets the clock on the progress of the Diné civilization. American capital, private property, and borders writhe into being on this alkali ground. They are put to the test. And they bring death.

The army assigns each Diné family a plot of land to farm. Clan relatives help each other to dig a seven-mile-long irrigation ditch that leads to other smaller irrigation ditches for fields of corn, melon, squash, and wheat. People starve every day. There are no shelters. Some dig holes in the banks of the river. Some throw sheepskins over poles between tree branches. The people drink from the dirty, alkali river and the waters make them sick. The soldiers watch. They are audience while the Navajos play a role that Carleton has assigned them. That role is the starving, savage Indian.

Carleton writes that the Diné are now "protégés of the United States—a people who, having given up their country, should be provided for by a powerful and Christian nation."[94]

The general has them. He asks the army for two million pounds of food, sent in five hundred thousand–pound installments.

The message comes clear from the wet, green world of Washington: there is a Civil War to win. The Navajos can wait. James Collins gets five hundred thousand pounds of flour and two thousand head of cattle out of Colorado.

The naadą́ą́' (corn) spirals up from three thousand acres of soil toward the sun. The tassels come out in the summer. Everything goes well. But the Diné have done something they would never do on their smaller farms in their settlements: they plant a large monoculture crop in one place. The swarm of moths that American agronomists call *Noctua pronuba* flaps to the field in the dark and lays its eggs. The eggs open under the ground and small fuzzy worms crawl up the stalks and inside the ears, eating deep inside the husks. The stalks grow tall and green. But the ears of *naadą́ą́'* rot from within. American agronomists would later call the insect "cutworm." The Diné had never seen it before. They have no name for it. It has come to them from that world of the East, its eggs perhaps even riding in the mix of seed corn given to them by the army.

The Diné farmers already understand this grim metaphor: the Americans help them to plant and three thousand acres of *naadą́ą́'* spring from the ground. And none of it can feed anybody. It is a hollow abundance that they have dared to worship.

The gods have abandoned them.

I have never seen Edison end a run by limping. Today he does. There is a lot of weight he's carrying.

We joke about how we're going to need to carry him king-style to the end in the plaza.

Edison knows the plaza will not be a finish line. There is no finish line. This is not a race. That's why Edison knows that no one will show up. Life will go on in the plaza. The Diné children sold as slaves will not get to relive their lives as free people with their families who would—or did—die for them. Pueblo women will still sell their jewelry on the blankets, submissive before the Palace of the Governors.

None of this will change when he finishes. The People never ran to win championships. They ran to survive.

Edison rubs his ankle and winces with pain.

"It's moving from my calf down to my ankle," he says. "I thought it was okay, but I think it's serious. It has a heartbeat."

That is—of course—if he does finish.

Carleton does not want the Navajo to return to the Confederate world beyond the forest. The Navajos would just go back to being hunted. He speaks these words and perhaps he is too insane to remember that he had just ordered them to be hunted. It is all a moral choice for Carleton: Do we let these people fight out their destiny? Or do we create utopias? And the gold. Ah, yes: the gold. If one looks into the pit of Carleton's conscience in the matter, they see mostly darkness. They feel movement of air. They hear dripping of water.

By the middle of winter, Diné men ride out ten or twenty miles to find logs and float them down the Pecos river for firewood. The government is not nearly as efficient. Congress appropriates one hundred thousand dollars for purchase of items. It becomes a corpse of money to be had. Mammon calls the feast and the merchants cluster. Through a dark magic, blankets worth $4.50 become $22.50 blankets. The merchants gorge on the difference. This happens with everything. Government agents pay out one hundred thousand dollars. Only thirty thousand dollars of goods arrive at Fort Sumner.

The Navajos do not know something. They do not know that the location Carleton has chosen for them puts them in a perfect place to absorb the violence of their old enemies, the Comanche, whose chiefs once swore to exterminate the Diné from the face of the earth.[95] Carleton knows this. He places them there and he knows it will be a killing ground and the bodies of the Diné will be a buffer against the Comanches' violence.

The women and children who walk to the river vanish and become slaves sold to Mexico. The sheep drop to Comanche arrows or are stolen away. The łįį́ (horse) become *puuku* (Comanche horse).

The soldiers have a solution: they hand out a few guns to the men to use while they herd sheep. The soldiers will not ride against the Comanches.

The Navajo warriors have a solution. They make headdresses of buffalo horns and paint their faces with the black and red war paint of the Comanche. They stalk over the walls of the fort and put arrows into five American soldiers and kill them before running into the shadows while calling Comanche war cries. The Americans scream vengeance and the Diné are their voice coaches.

The *Jau'di'* sees Santa Fe in the distance. Photo by Jim Kristofic.

This is the way of the Diné warriors, the men who dusted with corn pollen the paws of coyotes—the *mą'ii,* powerful tricksters and trouble-makers and roamers—so they could become true men. They can no longer roam. But they will make trouble. These men did not grow up being told to be like Jesus. If they had, they would probably be dead.

It is the afternoon run. Final day. The last thirteen miles.

Edison steps out of the Armada. He begins a few hundred yards back from where the neon-pink marker flaps in the shade of a Siberian elm that has grown up between gaps in the pavement at the edge of the highway. Cars scream past. Glass and steel cut the air. The light drums heat into the blacktop, into that color of death. And reverence.

Some Navajo people will say *Baaschlichiin* about the highway. The road is almost like a telephone line. *Baas'jíínii* or *Baasjíín. Eeyah.* "Oh the colors of the white, oh those sacred colors" when they travel the highway.

But these are roads of death. People die on these *all* the time.

It is a good way. It is a killer. Which will it be today?

Edison will use it to run downhill and push himself into the final stretch.

He has painted his right arm white and his left arm turquoise. His right leg is yellow and red. His left leg is black. The story is quiet. It is in the paint. It speaks of mountains, of a journey through the worlds, through forms and bodies, to this world with the help of the gods.

He runs past in his clearance-sale blue and white Nikes. His blue T-shirt with his daughter's illustration of him running flaps around his thin body.

I say to him, "*Yeegho, Jau'di'.*"

Edison runs past and whispers, "*Jau'di'. Hagoo.*" Follow me.

There is nothing else to say.

Carleton sends runners to Manuelito and tells him that, unless he and his band come in peacefully, they will be hunted down and killed with no mercy. Manuelito hides in the high country west of Zuni. He tells the runner, "My God and my Mother live here in the West. I will not leave them. Our people must never cross the three rivers to live—the Río Grande, the San Juan, and the Colorado. I cannot leave the Chuska Mountains where I was born. Here I shall remain. I have nothing to lose but my life, and that they can come and take whenever they please. But I will not go there."[96]

Carleton hears these words in Santa Fé. He orders Manuelito to be captured or killed. He guesses the chieftain's location from the runner's words and sends a band of Utes to do the job. Manuelito repels them. They come again after he has ridden out to Black Mesa. The Utes hit his band while he and his warriors are away on a hunting trip. The Utes decimate the people and take the survivors into slavery.

The Round Forest is gone now. The cottonwoods have been dropped for firewood. They have become poles and beams in adobe buildings for the soldiers at Fort Sumner. Now they will be used for the Diné to build their own adobe apartment homes. They will go up in uniform rows with wide streets between them, as any modern suburb. Trees will be planted for shade. It will become the best Indian village in the world "in point of beauty," according to the general who knows he has placed the Diné in front of the Comanche raiders who have previously wiped out entire Apache bands.[97]

If the Round Forest were a modern suburb—which it could be—it might be called Forest in the Round or Cottonwood Downs. Only it *is* a modern suburb, only it is 1864, only that the past is here now and Edison is running and the American general is talking and all the time he knows that he has placed the Diné in this place to absorb the bloodthirst of the Comanche so the New Mexican territory can increase its own wealth and the apartments go up and the chieftains refuse to live in them because they are men and braves and because they know they are houses of death and the apartments still go up in uniform rows and the shade trees planted at the edges of the parking lot say, "Come to the Forest. We will build a better world" and the rebels get hunted, the trees fall to the ax, the people absorb the violence of the wars, take what they can get, and all the while the white horse watches from the horizon and the wind streams in its mane and its tail and it is saying, "Run! Run for your life!" and Edison is running.

But in the magic thoughts of Carleton and the Americans, the Round Forest is still there. It is always there. And the smoking circle beckons. Come and sit with enemies on either side of you. You will be well. You will all be well and we will put you to sleep with knives into a ditch.

Edison runs to the exit to Cerrillos Road. We stop with him in the shade. Lorraine and Jay-Lynn emerge from the Armada in traditional velveteen shirts and long-strand turquoise necklaces. They have tied their hair back in *tsiyeeł* buns.

Edison takes water on his hat. His wrist. First two miles. He has to stretch using his chair. The ankle is hurting.

"I didn't think it was going to get this bad, honestly," he says. "But it started this morning in my calf muscle and spread down."

He takes off for the next two miles. I follow behind him in the Prius. It is obvious that Edison's ankle is bowed. It looks like it's going to snap.

The army does what every civilization has done since the first fields were planted along the Euphrates: it locks up the food. Commissary officers distribute cardboard ration tickets every other day. The army gets rid of the tickets, however, when they learn that Diné men can counterfeit them almost perfectly. They change to stamped metal discs to avoid the counterfeiting. They do not know that many Diné men are trained blacksmiths and easily forge the stamps and dies.[98] The Diné perform this act with no guilt. They know something that we do not: that money is its own lie.

By March 1856, more than nine thousand Diné and 350 Mescalero Apaches draw supplies. It becomes the single most successful program to feed people at that time.

The commissary counts almost three thousand counterfeit metal discs. The army solves the problem by importing tickets designed in Washington with such elaborate detail that no one can copy them. The people begin starving again on thin rations. They start to run.

Some wander to the New Mexico settlements they'd once robbed, to work as sheep-herding *peones*. Some leave because it is the only way they believe they can meet their gods again, that they might hear their prayers for health.

Within four months, Barboncito and Ganado Mucho's son—Ganado Blanco—have jumped the reservation. They know they are riding to a life of fugitive starvation.

Charles Sumner, the senator from Massachusetts who had been beaten with a cane at his writing desk by fellow senator Preston Brooks for arguing against slavery nine years before, rails against the process of "Indian slavery" in New Mexico. He convinces the president Andrew Johnson to suppress the practice of "Indian slavery."

He knows that perhaps five hundred people are enslaved in the capital of Santa Fé. He does not know that the governor of New Mexico keeps Navajo slaves.

Senator Dolittle sees it all at Bosque Redondo. He rides away in the July heat in that summer of 1865. It will take the United States government three years to move on the knowledge that the army is slowly starving people to death. This kind of delay is a foreign concept for the Diné. They are people of action.

The United States government system is designed to exhaust and strangle power in the individual, and only the shrewdest, most deceptive men who hold nothing sacred are permitted to handle the reins. It is a system designed to maximize profit by extraction, not to maximize survival.

The Americans know this and apply this logic to the Diné. They take Comanche land very near the trails the tribe uses to raid the ranches of southern New Mexico into Mexico. They have built an efficient kill box for the people and can tell history that it was all a tragic accident.

The newly recognized New Mexico citizens ignore Washington's chastisement over Indian slavery.

Manuel Chávez—who has moved on from the Fort Fauntleroy massacre to his seat as the territory's congressional delegate—keeps all of his slaves proudly.

Edison runs along Cerrillos road. People honk and drive past. The Armada pulls in to a nearby Comfort Inn. Edison sits and sips water.

Jason laughs. He says this is actually the Comfort Inn where they will be staying tonight.

"Try not to imagine that bed," he says as he pours ice water over Edison's back.

Edison's body is here but his mind is drifting. He studies the hotel's signage.

"They've got a pool," he says. "It's indoor."

Jason and Lorraine laugh, but they look at each other with worried eyes.

"I want a donut," Edison smiles. "A little donut. Do you remember that? 'How does he do it?!' It's that one from *Saturday Night Live*."

Lorraine and Jason shake their heads nervously. I start laughing with Edison. I remember it.

John Belushi stands before a high-jump bar. He is the decathlete champion in this comedy sketch and he is pushing toward a gold medal in the Olympics. His blue tank top, stitched with "USA" in red letters with white trim, stretches across his corpulent torso. He shakes his flabby arms. He wears a white elbow pad. His body looks like he could barely handle ten frames of bowling.

He runs at the bar. He clears seven feet. The announcer screams, "He's got it!"

Cut to the next scene. John Belushi runs down the final stretch of the 1,600 m. His body thunders and shakes. He sprints past the other runners. The announcer screams, "He's won the gold. Now he's going for the *world record!* He's making his move! There in the final turn! He's kicking it in! He's got it! A spectacular time! A new world's record! Unbelievable!"

John Belushi walks off the track in mock agony, waving an American flag. He's posted a mile-time of 4:11:30.

Cut to the next scene. John Belushi sits at a white table in front of a beige wall. He wears a black sweater over a white oxford shirt. On the table sits a white coffee mug and a white bowl filled with small, chocolate-frosted donuts. Next to the porcelain breakfast gear stands a yellow box covered with red and white lettering that reads "Donuts." A graphic of a track athlete sprints to victory. It looks like a Wheaties box.

Belushi smokes a cigarette. He looks soberly into the camera. "I logged a lot of miles training for that day. And I downed a lot of donuts. Little chocolate donuts. They taste good and they've got the sugar I need to get me going in the morning. That's why little chocolate donuts have been on *my* training table since I was a kid."

He takes a donut with the same hand holding the cigarette. He bites and chews through the smoke.

Cut to a shot of Belushi running in the pole vault. The announcer says, "Little Chocolate Donuts! The Donuts of Champions!"

In the first year we moved to the reservation, it was not easy. My mom demanded we laugh, and she bought us a VHS tape of the Best of John Belushi from *Saturday Night Live* from the Basha's Market in Window Rock. We must have watched that tape over three hundred times that year. It is still one of the funniest things I've seen.

Sadly, many Americans have taken Belushi's satire as actual training advice. So have many Diné. I laugh with Edison.

Theodore Dodd is appointed as agent to the Navajo at the Round

Forest. He emerges into history as a smallpox epidemic threatens to exterminate the tribe. Dodd knows this is not some tragic, perfect storm. The lesson is simple: cluster all the corn together and a moth you have never seen will leave you starving; cluster the people all together and a disease you have never seen will leave you dead. Dodd doesn't sleep in one place. Something moves his compassion.

Dodd receives permission to purchase a long list of agricultural tools, implements, and boxes of clothing to stave off genocide. When you see the Navajo at the Long Walk, at the Round Forest, some of you will see them standing behind a chain-link fence and barbed wire. That is historically inaccurate. But it is correct.

The territorial assembly turns against Carleton. The assembly—made up of men who own Navajo slaves—writes a letter to President Johnson to say that New Mexicans have been accused of attacks actually committed by Navajos. They are now part of America and it is a land of shapeshifters. In this land of fresh starts, the villains become the heroes. Up is down. Black is white.

The superintendent of Indian Affairs, A. Baldwin Norton, rides out. During the war with that Rope Thrower, Col. Christopher "Kit" Carson, and the Americans, Ganado Mucho is one of the last surrendering Navajo headmen. He does not travel with the first 1,443 people who surrendered at Fort Wingate in the late winter of 1864. Nor is he with the 3,200 who left Fort Defiance by the end of March. By July 8, 5,900 people are confined at Bosque Redondo next to Fort Sumner. Another thousand live in the depot at Fort Defiance.

Ganado Mucho—that son of the masterful Hopi runner—is not one of them. Instead, he walks his band down into the valley's sandy wash and follows it all the way south, through Hopi Country, to where it drains into the Little Colorado River and then disappears into the rocky labyrinth of the Grand Canyon.

He hears stories about the failed prayers and crops at Fort Sumner. The winter is brutal. The water is alkaline and nearly undrinkable. They start to call the place *Hweeldí*. The word comes to mean a "Place of Suffering."

Ganado Mucho hears these stories. His slow and rational mind begins to sprint. Winter is coming. A small storm has drifted over the canyons, spinning snowflakes that fall like chips of ice into the rock labyrinth where he and his people have lived for the past two years. Nobody has ever found them. But his sons have surrendered. Friends have taken the long march to Fort Sumner, and so have their families. He has long herds of sheep and goats, enough to feed thousands while the Americans decide what to do next. He can save lives, though it might cost him his own.

That fall of 1865, he decides to leave his secret stronghold and surrender himself and his relatives and his large herd of sheep and goats at Fort Wingate. Through an interpreter, he requests military escort for the women and children of his band, while the men follow behind with the life-saving herd of livestock. The American commander agrees.

During the trip to the fort, Ganado Mucho has not yet reached the army's camp near Albuquerque when New Mexicans attack and kidnap his two youngest daughters. American soldiers—some of whom have tried to rape one of his older daughters just days before—search for the lost children. They give up and say they have been sold into slavery in Mexico.

After arriving at Fort Sumner, Ganado Mucho finds his son, Ganado Blanco, and other starving clan members. They are thankful for the sheep and goats, whose meat soon sizzles over their small fires and runs hot into their stomachs. They make it through the winter. The wound of his grief for his lost daughters begins to heal. Then it is torn open that summer when Comanche raiders sweep through Bosque Redondo, steal two hundred horses, and kill his youngest son while he is herding the remaining sheep brought from their homeland. The army is supposed to protect them from Comanches. The army is not there. Ganado Mucho and other men are not allowed to have guns. They have only bows and arrows and shovels. They pick up the shovels and run at mounted archers. That is what you must understand about these men.

That summer, when the Superintendent of Indian Affairs, A. B. Norton, arrives to inspect the Bosque Redondo, Ganado Mucho sits with Norton and explains he has serious promises for the American.

"I have lost one of my sons and I am nearly crazy," he says through the army interpreter. "I feel very bad. How can we protect ourselves when our enemies are much better armed than we are? We want to go back to our own country . . . we want to go back there the same as we are here. The land here will never be as good as our own country. The government does not supply us with wood here, and we had plenty there. If the government would put us on a reservation in our own country and keep us the same as here within boundaries, the government would see how we work. We think we were born to live in our old country . . . we think we were not born to live here."

Ten days later, Ganado Mucho's brother rides in and reports that Manuelito is still hiding, but he is wounded and weak. The month of September comes and Manuelito and twenty-three of his followers ride into Fort Wingate. Their clothing hangs in rags. They have no weapons. The forty-eight-year-old chieftain makes no florid speech. He makes no promise to fight no more forever. His rage is enough when he accepts the shackles. Twelve days after Manuelito arrives, Carleton is reassigned to Louisiana.

Edison finishes the two miles. His ankle is bowed to where I fear he will step it into the concrete. He sits in the chair and spits dry.

A small car pulls up behind the Prius and a Diné woman steps out. She runs up to Lorraine and gives her money for Edison's GoFundMe page, where he is raising money for the educational programs of Western National Parks Association. She has followed John Belushi's training advice and her body quakes with fat. She could not have run two miles. But she wants to give something.

Edison shakes her hand and thanks her. She gets back in the car.

He sips water. "Man," he says. "Whose idea *was this?*"

Lorraine and Jason laugh.

The plants keep dying. The Río Pecos shrinks to a trickle. The surviving pumpkins, beans, and peas are killed by hailstorms in the late summer. What do you think? If you know the corn songs and the rain songs and you sit in wet clothes at the doorway of your adobe hut and the hail cracks and falls to the sand and a hailstone lands by your brown foot and begins to melt and glow a perfect ice sphere the same shape as the musket balls you have seen rip through the bodies of children and that you have loaded and sent through the bodies of teenage shepherds during a raid for livestock, then what do you think then, when you see the grass chewed into the dirt until the ribs on your cattle begin to show? When the soldiers appear with guns and force you to work the fields? When your neighbors take the cattle and sheep south off the reservation and the soldiers show up and open fire? Your neighbors fight back and kill five soldiers and almost kill four others. Do you stay?

You leave. You run.

The superintendent has plans. He calls Manuelito, Ganado Mucho, and nine other *naat'áanii* to Santa Fé. He tells them that the wise butcher Ulysses S. Grant has transferred their fates from the military to the civilian Indian department. This seems like good news.

While the chieftains are gone, over two hundred Comanche ride down on the Navajo camps around Fort Sumner. It is a slaughter. The only weapons the men have are shovels, mattocks, and knives. They pick them up. They run at the mounted Comanche, who fire arrows and bullets from their galloping horses.

The Navajos run after them for sixteen miles. These are men who would wake before dawn and run to the east in the morning.

The commander of the fort writes: "I must express my admiration of their courage and daring."

But their valiant spirits cannot run down the strange bureaucracies born of the quill, the ink pot, the paper press, and the creak of the wooden writing desk. The military tries to write laws to hold them.

Parents send their children to the elementary school Carleton establishes in the suburb of Fort Sumner. He does this to pull the Diné away from "their savage desire to roam about and lead a life of idleness." The children attend so they can receive a meal ticket. Once the army takes away the meal ticket, the children stop coming.[99]

The soldiers are mostly Anglo men. Most of the Diné captives are women. The two races live together. They strike a deal and that deal is food for sex. In the Diné creation story, the many forms of the People move through several worlds. One thing that keeps them moving is the proclivity they have for committing adultery and other unhealthy sexual acts with the wives of their hosts.

The flesh does not lie and syphilis tells its story of rashes, hair loss, and partial blindness. The soldiers stationed at Fort Sumner soon post the highest rate of venereal disease in the army.[100]

Manuelito rides through Bosque Redondo to see if it is any good for his people. While he is there, he sees children hunched over the manure piles in the corrals, picking out corn undigested by the soldiers' horses. Then they eat it.

He has seen enough. He rides out under cover of darkness that night back to Fort Fauntleroy.

Edison is supposed to stop at the intersection of St. Michael's Avenue and Cerrillos. But he keeps going. He runs an extra mile. He walks to the Armada and favors his ankle.

"It's about to go," he says as Lorraine rubs his calf muscle. "If it goes? That snap? It's not good."

He sips water.

"Whose idea *was* this?" I say.

Edison smiles. "How does he *do it?!*" And we are laughing over the shared image of a husky John Belushi sprinting past whippet-thin track athletes.

When you must suffer, you must laugh.

Cadete—that Mescalero chief who had told Carson his people were men and braves—perhaps sees to the root of the Round Forest, the suburban grid, the Jesus and the forgetting and the nightmare of the American Dream. He speaks to an army officer one day and his words strike the officer so soundly that the officer has them printed in a magazine.

"Let me tell you what we think," Cadete says. "You begin when you are little to work hard. After you get to be men, you build big houses, big towns, and everything else in proportion. Then, after you have got them all, you die and leave them behind. Now, we call that slavery. You are slaves from the time you begin to talk until you die; but we are free as air. The Mexicans and others work for us. Our wants are few and easily supplied. The river, the wood, and plain yield all that we require. We will not be slaves; nor will we send our children to your schools, where they only learn to become like yourselves."[101]

In April 1865, Grant and Lee sign the armistice at Appomattox Court House. The Civil War slows down to a speed where it is barely noticed and pushes on today.

Senator Dolittle from Wisconsin travels to New Mexico territory two months later to study the United States policy on Indians. He interviews Carson at his home in Taos. He asks the battle-scarred man why the New Mexicans are so opposed to the Navajos being kept at the Round Forest.

Carson says it is because the slave markets in Santa Fé and Taos are drying up with no more Navajos to hunt. He says the New Mexicans "cannot prey on them as formerly."

The army begins to fatigue of Bosque Redondo. It is costing the taxpayers a million dollars a year and the Diné do not seem to want to become the kind of Americans the army wants.[102]

The Round Forest swallows three thousand Diné. That is a kill rate of one out of every three captives held there.

In the spring of 1868, the Diné men refuse to plant. There is no longer any point. There are only the rations. And they spend their days conserving energy, waiting for food outside the fort.

During this time, there is a story that the chieftain and medicine singer Barboncito walks out with the people in the sagebrush to do a Bead Way. Each man and woman take up rocks in their hands. They spread out in a circle more than a mile wide. They clack those rocks together and walk into each other. The circle shrinks. Rabbits and doves flee before the people. And so does a coyote. The people walk up on the coyote until the *mą'ii* relaxes and submits to Barboncito and his men. They sing and chant and hold the coyote down. Barboncito places a bead of white shell in the coyote's mouth, rubs the animal's white throat, and makes him swallow it.

Then they let the coyote up and they back away. They watch and their songs go quiet. The coyote sneezes and trots out of the circle to the west. Barboncito announces this means the Diné will also be going west. Home.

The Diné asked to go home. *Mą'ii*—that trickster, that survivor, whose paws the corn pollen dusted before dropping into the medicine pouch that made someone a man—shows them the way. That is the story they tell, that it was all finished in beauty.

There is another story.

I was out at the sheep camp near Piñon, Arizona, in the first winter I had moved back to New Mexico. My *chéí* was there. His muscles had started to fade in his face. One of his eyes had developed a cataract and glowed dull blue at the edge. The wind lifted and dropped his white hair. I had herded sheep for him as a boy. I had weeded his garden. I impressed him with my understanding of the Holy Bible. His father was a respected medicine man who knew the Beauty Way chant.

He was a man who had taken the iron road, as a railroad worker. He had tattoos on his forearms. He spoke good English. He had seen the world.

I told him I was starting a writing project about the Hero Twins.

"The twins," he said. He looked to the north. "During the Long Walk, a woman gave birth to twins. The people took them and killed them, they say. It was a human sacrifice to make sure the People went free. They say that's how people got back home."

I have checked this story with several traditional people. They say it is true. Take your pick. Maybe they both happened. Nothing changes the truth: those choices hover before us now as they have before any people: Do we use the past to have a future? Or do we sacrifice the future to have a present? Do we ask the Great Ones to put blood into our children or do we paint the gods with our children's blood? Do we play Zeus or do we play Cronus? Do we want to be part of life or death?

If this story is true—and I believe it is—then it means that the Diné in the Round Forest become a people who know their children are born to die. How long does it take for them to believe this? How long do we have?

Edison dances the two miles on a bent ankle. His gait has changed, but he is still running fast. He kicks his own ankle and stumbles. He does not fall and runs past The Pantry restaurant on Cerrillos.

"Two more," he says. "How does *he do it?*"

He stands. He shakes the black rattle. It is a comfort. It takes it. It takes the pain. He pushes on. The traffic screams past. It is a sunny Sunday afternoon. A woman taps at her phone at a bus stop while Edison runs past her. She doesn't notice. He might as well not be there.

Jason folds up the chair. "You know, I notice something," he says. "Every time he stops—every time—he's never out of breath."

It is a date called May 28, 1868, when William Tecumseh Sherman arrives in a convoy to the Round Forest. Dodd gives him a status report: 7,304 people remain on the Reservation. Nine hundred escaped. Probably more than 2,000 people died. He has no count for how many were stolen into slavery by Comanche and New Mexicans.[103]

The chieftains select Barboncito to speak for them. He sits with Sherman—that tight-lipped man who had set fire to Dixieland—and tells him he looks at Sherman as a spirit and speaks to him as though he were a spirit.

The men have it out. They finish negotiating June 1, 1868, in the Moon of the Small Leaves. Twenty-nine chieftains sign, including Barboncito, Armijo, Manuelito, Ganado Mucho, and Delgadito. The treaty establishes a world of borders and the Diné take oaths to believe in borders unsung in any of their prayers. The army does what it has proven adept at doing. It takes away their country.

The north border ends at Fort Defiance. The east border ends at Bear Springs. The west border ends at Canyon de Chelly. The south border is decided by whatever murdering ranchers decide to shoot at Navajo teenagers herding the family's sheep.

The Americans buy peace. For two years, they will give the Navajo seeds and agricultural implements, livestock and corn, cloth for making clothing for the next ten years. The Diné will send their children to school. They will become captives.

The treaty says nothing about the return of Navajo captives. Sherman improvises and tells the *naat'áanii* that he has recently finished fighting a great war against slavery. Slavery is outlawed. He says they can apply to the judges of the civil courts and land commissioners to get their relatives back. One of Sherman's colonels asks Barboncito how many Navajos are held captive by the New Mexicans. The thin old man says it is over half the tribe.[104]

That same week, Kit Carson lies on the floor of his doctor's quarters at Fort Lyon. He spits up blood forced by an aneurysm in his neck and chest. It is so painful that Carson asks the doctor for so much painkilling opium and chloroform that the doctor fears it will kill him.

Carson's wife had died from an infection a few weeks before. She was forty years old.

The moon does not become full again before Carson dies coughing blood in the doctor's arms.

Edison coughs and sips water. The plaza is two miles away.

"Gotta get it," he says. "Something out there."

He smiles and Lorraine wets his red bandana.

"Okay," he says. He shakes the black rattle. "I'm going, guys. Don't worry about me. I'm done."

Edison runs toward the plaza and passes out of our sight.

On the way, he stops for twenty seconds in front of the State Capitol.

He walks ten steps from the East to the West. He takes his cap off. He gently lowers his head. He speaks softly.

"*H'át'íish biniiye'?*" What was the purpose of this? Why did this happen?

He ran 330 miles to do that. No one sees it.

Then he runs to the plaza.

We negotiate the tight streets of Santa Fe and find a place to park. Lorraine walks out of the Armada carrying a pair of scissors.

"What's that for?" I ask.

"For Edison," she says. "For what he's going to say."

We walk to the bustling plaza. Western National Parks Association has set up a booth. A young woman weaves at a cottonwood loom. She is part of the ceremony of the run. The weaving of a new *ya'sikaad.*

Edison is already standing on the bandstand in the center of the plaza. Western National Parks Association dignitaries surround him. They give him space and pass him the microphone.

When Edison first told me about the run, he spoke of stopping at the Roundhouse in Santa Fé, at the state capitol. I saw him walking on painted limbs into the state assembly, the silk-suited, bolo-tied representatives quieted in the presence of the Return of the *Jau'di'*. The black rattle shakes in his white-painted hand. He limps to the central podium. Dust motes drift in the shafts of sunlight. The descendants of the slavers hold their breath. The fat of their chins quivers. Some of them stand in respectful silence. They are descendants of the Diné. The runner has the message. And so much of the message has followed him. They are all here.

The white horse trots into the assembly. He stamps and snorts. Its whinny is warning and declaration.

The woman at Where Two Fell Off clutches hands with the Mexican soldier who came to kill her family. They walk down the aisle as bridegroom and bride. Her woven dress shakes sand to her bare feet.

The twenty-four chieftains walk in together. They have left their ditch at Jémez. Their silver necklaces clink against their bare chests. Their dark faces brood beneath their headbands. The blood from the knife wounds in their chests stains the white bands of their blankets. One holds a pipe and it smokes sweet tobacco.

The Navajo warriors in masks of mountain lion scalps brandish their lances and keep fingers at their bowstrings as they walk between the desks. Some go to guard the exits. No funny stuff. So many more are arriving.

They keep coming. Every grandmother left with food to die alone in the freezing night. Every child left to sleep in the earth. A group of men walk in with bloody shirts. Comanche arrows quiver in their bodies. These men laugh and joke with each other as they approach the podium. Zarcillos Largos walks between staffers holding their cell phones. His sinews have regrown. He lays his silver-headed cane on a table.

Narbona rides into the crowd, his proud face shining like a portrait of George Washington. His wounds bleed like stigmata and he whoops as flecks of blood mist into his long white hair. He flicks his blood onto white blouses and black suits. The representatives cringe. The people come and they come and they come until thousands fill the Roundhouse.

Edison goes to the mic. He shakes the black rattle. That is what he has to say. That is the message.

We are still here. We have survived. There will always be Diné. We will always be here.

The people are the message.

And the white horse leads them out. Behind them trail greasy, muddy bear tracks on the carpet.

Jim Cook, the executive director of the Western National Parks Association, takes the mic and thanks Edison for all he has done. He is an inspiration.

Lorraine hands Edison the scissors.

He hands Edison the mic. People clap. "In the traditional way, we confirm our investment," Edison says. "Our ideas. Our dreams. Our world. Our faith base. And you're going to see one."

People expect more of a speech. They expect to hear the Message. But this is not a speech. This is a dance. A ceremony.

What can Edison possibly *say?* He decides to speak without words.

In the days of Narbona, Zarcillos Largos, and Ganado Mucho, a man mourned the loss of a relative by cutting his own hair.

Edison pulls his long hair back into a ponytail and takes up the scissors. He cuts his hair.

People don't know if they should clap. Some do. Those who know stand quiet.

Edison holds out the black rattle to Jim Cook, the WNPA executive director. He makes the rattle a gift to Jim and tells Jim he can do anything he wants with it.

I walk up the bandstand. I bring Edison a Tupperware container of fruit salad from a woman in the crowd. I hand him a cold can of Coca-Cola.

"*Ahéhee*'," he says. Thank you.

He sips the Coke. He sucks and chews at each piece of melon and pineapple carefully. He doesn't speak. Edison once said that it is easy to change things when they are given by the voice. You can change the words by the voice. But you cannot change actions. To do what he has done has been a teaching device. He was dancing in the road. It was a classroom setting.

"As you run, your mind starts to get simple," Edison said on that first day of the run. "You'll see. When we get farther, start asking me some math problems." He laughed.

I consider my own math problem for this still point on the plaza. For Edison to run a mile, he had to take about 1,600 strides to push himself forward. I had learned from biologist and runner Berndt Heinrich that on each stride, most runners push themselves three inches into the air.[105] This means that for each mile, Edison pushed himself 400 total feet into the air. Everyone knows Edison traveled 330 miles forward through space to reach this place. But not everyone might contemplate that he also traveled almost 25 miles into the sky, well beyond the boundary of the stratosphere, above the clouds. Where the Great Ones live and watch and speak.

As he sucks down the fruit salad, I don't ask him anything. His feet are on the earth. His mind is up there, with the Great Ones. The Ones who greet you with *Yá'áát'ééh*.

When he finished his first ultrarun, Edison turned and heard a voice from the Great Ones. The voice told him, "You are on the Rainbow Path."

I wonder if he is there now.

This is not the place to ask him. I keep my math to myself.

"Come on," he says. "I want you to meet my mom."

Edison's mother is no taller than my sternum. Her eyes rim with a blue sheen when they look you over. She is mostly blind now. She knows as much English as most Americans know Navajo. Very little.

Edison said one night he was driving back to Santa Fe and decided to stop to visit his mom at their family home on the other side of the mountain at Springstead. That night, he sat on the couch in the living room in the dark, watching an NBA playoff game on the TV. His mom sat in her chair. The channel cut away from the game to a commercial break and the Geico Gecko appeared and told America they could save 15 percent on car insurance.

His mom asked Edison in Navajo, "Son, is that lizard really talking *on the television?*"

"No, Mom," Edison said. "It's just a computer-generated image. That's not a real lizard."

Edison watched until the Lakers won. Then he fell asleep on the couch.

His mom made him coffee the next morning. But something bothered him about the way his mother spoke the night before. Something that she said about the lizard.

He was driving east on Route 40 when it hit him. His mom had been surprised to see a lizard talking on the television. But she had *not* been surprised to see a lizard *talking.* She had seen that before.

"And I said to myself, 'Holy shit! My mom is hearing the spirit world,'" Edison said.

Lorraine explains in Navajo who I am and why I was with Edison during the run.

Edison's mom looks me over. She tells Lorraine I have a Navajo name now. She tells me what it is.

"There it is," Lorraine says. "So don't forget it."

I know I won't.

The crowd begins to break up and the band begins to play. Visitors walk to the Western National Parks Association booth set up next to the bandstand. People walk to their loved ones. They pose for photographs. Edison leaves to rest.

People are packed and ready to leave by June 18, 1868. The column of walkers stretches ten miles. Dodd, his wife, and two children bump along in a wagon. Four companies of cavalry ride back. They cover ten to twelve miles a day. But I like to think some of the young men scout ahead. Some of them run.

The runners are the first to see the sloping, blue pyramid of *Tsoodził* (Mt. Taylor). They know they are in their own country.

An old man who had survived said, "When we saw the top of the mountain from Albuquerque, we wondered if it was our mountain, and we felt like talking to the ground, we loved it so."[106]

Edison resting after reaching the Palace of the Governor's in the plaza at Santa
Fe, New Mexico, from Spider Rock. 330 miles. Photo by Gabriela Campos.

And what do the People say? What does the ground say back? What
voices speak in us? Diné chieftains like Ganado Mucho—that runner,
that son of the Hopi runner—knew two voices spoke our actions. Our
living spirit. And our *ch'įįndii*.

Which one of these voices spoke freedom for the Diné at the Round
Forest? Was it the Bead Way and the Coyote? Was it the deaths of the
sacrificed twins? Perhaps the Round Forest followed them back. Perhaps
they are still living in it. Is the blue mountain talking or is the uranium
hissing under the earth? Is *Tsoodził* speaking in lightning and thunder?
Or is the skull screaming from the leather seat of the motorcycle? Maybe
only Coyote knows for sure.

What is the Message? What did Edison want to say? Perhaps it is
something in that voice of our living spirit. The sound of yellow pollen
opening in the dawn, a sudden expression of determined life and beauty.
You think of that and you say, "*Sąʼah naagháí bikeʼhózhǫ́.*" The Long
Life. The Beautiful Life. Mother Earth. Father Sky.

Perhaps it is the sound of the breath leaving the runner's mouth.

To hear that message, perhaps you get a rattle. Perhaps you tie on your running shoes. You go forward in stride. Maybe in the dawn. Maybe whenever you have time. But you create that rhythm. Your body creates the charge. The rattle shakes. It is a comfort.

You listen to this.

You find it by running. The run is the prayer. Your feet drum to Mother Earth. Your breath chants to Father Sky. But it has nothing to do with running.

Listen to the rattle.

That is the message.

When you hear that sound, drop to the earth. Talk to the ground. Love it so.

You will be where it starts and continues. You will be in the prayers.

Ts'aa', the Navajo basket for prayers. Ganado, Arizona. Photo by Edison Eskeets.

Notes

1. Sung by David Frésquez, age sixty-seven, from Ranchos de Taos, for the John D. Robb Archives of Southwest Music (Center for Southwest Research, Zimmerman Library, UNM).

2. Raymond Friday Locke, *The Book of the Navajo* (Los Angeles: Mankind Press, Inc., 1992).

3. George P. Hammond and Agapito Rey, *The Rediscovery of New Mexico 1580–1594; the Explorations of Chamuscado, Espejo, Casteno de Sosa, Morlette, and Leyoa de Bonilla and Humana* (Albuquerque: University of New Mexico Press, 1966).

4. Frank McNitt, *Navajo Wars: Military Campaigns, Slave Raids, and Reprisals* (Albuquerque: University of New Mexico Press, 1972).

5. David Brugge, *Navajo Times,* May 19, 1966.

6. Gaspar Pérez de Villagrá, *Historia de la Nueva Mexico* (1610), Canto 26.

7. Charles Lummis, *Mesa, Cañon, and Pueblo* (New York: Century, 1925), 189.

8. Fray Alonso de Benavides, *The Memorial to the King of Fray Alonso de Benavides, 1630* (Mishawaka, IN: Palala Press, 2015).

9. Juan Armando Niel, "Apuntamientos que a las memorias del P. Fray Gerónimo de Zárate Salmerón hizo el P. Juan Armando Niel de la Compañía de Jesús" (1710), in *Documentos para servir a la historia de Nuevo México, 1528–1778* (Madrid: José Porrúa Turranzas, 1965).

10. Locke, *The Book of the Navajo,* 179.

11. James F. Brooks, *Captives and Cousins: Slavery, Kinship, and Community in the Southwest Borderlands* (Chapel Hill: University of North Carolina Press, 2002), 93.

12. Ramón Gutiérrez, *When Jesus Came, the Corn Mothers Went Away: Marriage, Sexuality, and Power in New Mexico, 1500–1846* (Stanford: Stanford University Press, 1991).

13. Enrique R. Lamadrid, *Hermanitos Comanchitos: Indo-Hispano Rituals of Captivity and Redemption* (Albuquerque: University of New Mexico Press, 2003), 30.

14. McNitt, *Navajo Wars,* 21.

15. Ernest Wallace and E. Adamson Hoebel, *The Comanches: Lords of the South Plains,* Civilization of the American Indian Series, vol. 34 (Norman: University of Oklahoma Press, 1952).

16. Raymond Friday Locke, *The Book of the Navajo,* 5th ed. (Los Angeles: Mankind Publishing Company, 1992), 181.

17. Locke, *Book of the Navajo,* 161.

18. Locke, *Book of the Navajo,* 183.

19. Brugge, *Navajo Times,* May 19, 1966.

20. Berndt Heinrich, *Why We Run: A Natural History* (New York: Ecco Publishers, 2002), 65–67.

21. Heinrich, *Why We Run,* 83. The authors also gratefully acknowledge the work of John A. Kissane, "The Navajo Are Still Here—And He Ran 330 Miles to Prove It," *Runner's World,* September 5, 2018.

22. Peter Nabakov, *Indian Running: Native American History and Tradition* (Santa Fe: Ancient City Press, 1981), 22.

23. Nabakov, *Indian Running,* 22.

24. Nabakov, *Indian Running,* 22.

25. Arlyssa Becenti, "Hubbell Trader Runs to Honor Those Who Had No Choice," *The Navajo Times,* May 24, 2018, A4. The authors also gratefully acknowledge the work of Cindy Yurth, "Thoreau: On the Road to Hope," *Navajo Times,* May 8, 2014, and all of her monumental Chapter Series for the *Navajo Times.*

26. Pliny Earle Goddard, *Navajo Texts. Anthropological Papers of the American Museum of Natural History,* vol. 34 (New York: American Museum of Natural History, 1933).

27. Locke, *Book of the Navajo,* 190.

28. Dora Ortiz Vásquez, *Enchanted Temples of Taos: My Story of Rosario* (Santa Fe: Rydal Press, 1975).

29. Hampton Sides, *Blood and Thunder: The Epic Story of Kit Carson and the Conquest of the American West* (New York: Anchor Books, 2006), 335.

30. Locke, *Book of the Navajo,* 202.

31. Sides, *Blood and Thunder,* 167.

32. Locke, *Book of the Navajo,* 206.

33. Locke, *Book of the Navajo,* 206.

34. Locke, *Book of the Navajo,* 209.

35. Locke, *Book of the Navajo,* 210.

36. Locke, *Book of the Navajo,* 213–14.

37. Judy Pasternak, *Yellow Dirt: A Poisoned Land and the Betrayal of the Navajos* (New York: Free Press, 2011).

38. Locke, *Book of the Navajo,* 253

39. Locke, *Book of the Navajo,* 258.

40. Locke, *Book of the Navajo,* 259.

41. Nabakov, *Indian Running,* 88.

42. Locke, *Book of the Navajo,* 261.

43. Locke, *Book of the Navajo,* 271.

44. Locke, *Book of the Navajo,* 275.

45. Locke, *Book of the Navajo*, 276.
46. Locke, *Book of the Navajo*, 278.
47. Locke, *Book of the Navajo*, 284.
48. Locke, *Book of the Navajo*, 288.
49. Locke, *Book of the Navajo*, 295.
50. Locke, *Book of the Navajo*, 297.
51. Locke, *Book of the Navajo*, 299.
52. Locke, *Book of the Navajo*, 300.
53. Locke, *Book of the Navajo*, 300.
54. Locke, *Book of the Navajo*, 306.
55. Locke, *Book of the Navajo*, 309.
56. Locke, *Book of the Navajo*, 312.
57. Locke, *Book of the Navajo*, 313.
58. Locke, *Book of the Navajo*, 314.
59. Locke, *Book of the Navajo*, 315.
60. Locke, *Book of the Navajo*, 317.
61. Locke, *Book of the Navajo*, 315.
62. Locke, *Book of the Navajo*, 318–19.
63. Locke, *Book of the Navajo*, 324.
64. Locke, *Book of the Navajo*, 327.
65. Locke, *Book of the Navajo*, 327.
66. Locke, *Book of the Navajo*, 330.
67. Locke, *Book of the Navajo*, 331.
68. Locke, *Book of the Navajo*, 332.
69. Locke, *Book of the Navajo*, 333.
70. Heinrich, *Why We Run*, 158.
71. Locke, *Book of the Navajo*, 334.
72. Locke, *Book of the Navajo*, 335.
73. Sung by David Frésquez, age sixty-seven, from Ranchos de Taos, for the John D. Robb Archives of Southwest Music (Center for Southwest Research, Zimmerman Library, UNM).
74. Locke, *Book of the Navajo*, 336.
75. Locke, *Book of the Navajo*, 337.
76. Locke, *Book of the Navajo*, 337.
77. Sides, *Blood and Thunder*, 158.
78. Locke, *Book of the Navajo*, 384.
79. Lamadrid, *Hermanitos Comanchitos*.
80. Locke, *Book of the Navajo*, 351.
81. Locke, *Book of the Navajo*, 352.
82. Locke, *Book of the Navajo*, 352–53.
83. Locke, *Book of the Navajo*, 353.

84. Sides, *Blood and Thunder*, 423.

85. Locke, *Book of the Navajo*, 356

86. Broderick H. Johnson, ed., *Navajo Stories of the Long Walk Period* (Phoenix, AZ: Arrowhead Press, Inc., printed for Navajo Community College Press, 1973), 125–26.

87. Sides, *Blood and Thunder*, 422.

88. Lawrence C. Kelly, *Navajo Roundup: Selected Correspondence of Kit Carson's Expedition against the Navajo, 1863–1865* (Boulder: Pruett Press, 1970).

89. Locke, *Book of the Navajo*, 357.

90. Broderick, *Navajo Stories*. From Akinabah Burbank (Alk'inanibaa' Burbank) of Valley Store, Arizona. She is from *Táchii'nii* (Red Streak Running Into the Water) clan.

91. Locke, *Book of the Navajo*, 359–60.

92. Locke, *Book of the Navajo*, 363.

93. Locke, *Book of the Navajo*, 363.

94. Sides, *Blood and Thunder*, 447.

95. Locke, *Book of the Navajo*, 368

96. Locke, *Book of the Navajo*, 363.

97. Locke, *Book of the Navajo*, 370.

98. Locke, *Book of the Navajo*, 371.

99. Sides, *Blood and Thunder*, 455.

100. Sides, *Blood and Thunder*, 456.

101. Locke, *Book of the Navajo*, 475.

102. Sides, *Blood and Thunder*, 476.

103. Locke, *Book of the Navajo*, 382.

104. Locke, *Book of the Navajo*, 386.

105. Heinrich, *Why We Run*, 158.

106. Paul Horgan, *Great River: The Rio Grande in North American History*, vol. 2 (Middletown, CT: Wesleyan University Press, 1984), 333.